Ben A. Russell, CFP®, CRPC™, APMA™, CEPA™

# THE INFINITE TEAM

Building a Purpose-Driven Financial Advisory Practice That Outlasts Your Career

INFLUENTIAL ADVISOR
MEDIA

Published by
**Influential Advisor Media**

DISCLAIMER:
This book contains the opinions and ideas of the author and is intended for educational and informational purposes only. Careful attention has been paid to ensure the accuracy of the information presented, but the author cannot assume responsibility for the validity or consequences of its use.

The content of this book should not be construed as specific financial, investment, tax, or legal advice. Every individual's financial situation is unique, and readers should consult with qualified professionals who can evaluate their specific circumstances, needs, and goals before making any financial decisions.

The examples, case studies, and scenarios presented in this book are for illustrative purposes only and do not guarantee or predict any particular outcome. Past performance is not indicative of future results. Individual results will vary.

No reader should act or refrain from acting based solely on the information contained in this book without first seeking appropriate professional advice. Any use of the information found in this book is the sole responsibility of the reader. The author, publisher, and any affiliated entities disclaim any liability for actions taken or not taken based on the contents of this book.

# CONTENTS

DR. JON RANDALL

# FOREWORD

I HAVE SPENT THE last two decades studying what separates the best from the rest. Not just the most successful by the industry's usual measures like the biggest AUM, the highest revenue, the top ranking on some leaderboard; I mean the advisors who are genuinely thriving. The ones who are doing the work they were built to do, serving families at the level they deserve, building something they are proud of and still making it home for dinner.

I have coached and consulted with many hundreds of financial advisory practices. I have sat across from advisors at every stage of the career arc: from the eager beginner dialing for dollars to the grizzled veteran who built something remarkable and is trying to figure out what comes next. And in all of that work, one pattern shows up again and again. The same thing that made them great is slowly destroying them.

The drive. The discipline. The belief that if they just work hard enough, long enough, they can serve everyone well. It's the mindset that built their practice. And it's the mindset that has them booked solid for six months, missing their kid's activities, and quietly dreading the thought of another decade doing this the same way. Ben Russell calls this the Solo Practitioner's Paradox. I call it the primary constraint of our industry. Different language. Same painful reality.

My background is in performance psychology. Before I founded eXtraordinary Financial Advisors, I spent years studying how elite performers in any field, athletes, surgeons, executives, reach and sustain peak performance. The research is clear on one point that our industry consistently ignores: no high performer sustains elite output alone, indefinitely, without a team and a system built to support them.

Every elite athlete has coaches, training staff, and teammates. Every great surgeon has a surgical team. Every top executive has a leadership bench. The idea that a financial advisor, someone responsible for the retirement security, the legacy, and the financial wellbeing of hundreds of families, should do it all themselves is not a badge of honor. It is a structural flaw. And it produces exactly the outcomes you would expect: capacity ceilings, service degradation, burnout, and practices that disappear the moment their founder steps back.

The framework I use in my work is based on the Theory of Constraints which identifies the single bottleneck limiting a system's growth, then focuses every resource on removing it. In most advisory practices, that bottleneck is the advisor themselves. Their time. Their attention. Their identity. They have become the ceiling of their own practice. What Ben has written is the most honest and practical roadmap I have seen for removing that constraint. Not by working harder. By building differently.

What sets this book apart is that Ben doesn't start with org charts or compensation structures or technology stacks. He starts with purpose. In my years coaching advisors, I have seen more practice-building initiatives fail from a lack of clarity about "why" than from a lack of skill in the "how." Advisors hire too fast, because they need relief. They build teams around their own preferences, not around shared values. They create structures that are really just solo practices with more people in the room. Then they wonder why the culture doesn't hold, why junior advisors don't stay, why clients still think of it as "your" firm and not "our" firm.

Ben spent a year, an entire year, doing the values work before touching an org chart. Most advisors won't believe that. Some will think it sounds soft. But here's what I know from the psychology of high performance: the teams that last, the cultures that scale, the organizations that outlast any single individual are all built on a foundation of shared meaning. Ben's Seventy-Five Year Promise isn't a marketing slogan. It's a strategic commitment that forces the right questions. What kind of team does it take to make a promise like that? What kind of leaders? What kind of pipeline? What kind of succession? When you start with that promise, everything downstream gets clearer.

To the financial advisor who is reading this and already looking for the exit. You know who you are. You have been in the business fifteen, maybe twenty-five years. You have built something real. But you are tired in a way a good night's sleep doesn't fix. You are thinking about an exit (a sale, a merger, a slow fade) because you can't imagine doing this the way you have been doing it for another decade. What you are planning to exit isn't the profession. It's the structure. And the structure can change. That's what Ben is really offering here. Not a checklist for scaling. A different way of thinking about what you are building and why. He went from 225 clients to 100. He works with fewer families, at a deeper level, with more impact. He is walking El Camino in Spain this fall because the team he built doesn't need him to be in the office 100% of the time. That's not a retirement story. That's a design story. You can build that. Or, if building isn't right for you, Ben will help you find the team worth joining. Either path leads somewhere better than where you are right now.

The financial advisory profession is at an inflection point. Industry data on advisor shortages and the widening gap between elite teams and solo practices is not a blip. It is a structural shift. The industry is maturing. Margins are compressing. Clients are more sophisticated and more demanding. The solo practitioner model is already at its limits for most advisors and is becoming less tenable with every passing year. The advisors who build or join elite, values-driven teams now will not just survive that shift. They will be the ones families choose. They will be the ones who attract the next generation of great advisors. They will be the ones still doing meaningful work in their sixties because the infrastructure they built makes that possible. The advisors who wait will run out of runway.

Ben Russell is one of the most thoughtful practitioners I have encountered in this work. He is not writing from theory, he is writing from the inside of a transformation that took years, cost more than he expected, and gave him more than he imagined. The Teaching Hospital model, the Seventy-Five Year Promise, the discipline to spend a full year on values before touching structure. These are not concepts Ben borrowed. They are things he lived. Read this book the way Ben built his team. Slowly. Deliberately. With the willingness to ask yourself the hard questions he puts in front of you. And then build something worth building.

*Dr. Jon Randall*
*Founder, eXtraordinary Financial Advisors Author,*
*The eXtraordinary Financial Advisor Practice*

DR. SHAYNE TRACY FOUNDER

# FOREWORD

LOOKING BACK ON THAT first phone conversation, I am not surprised by what Ben has accomplished. The qualities that were evident then (vision, curiosity, determination, intelligence, humility, and a deep commitment to serving others) have continued to define his leadership journey. What began as an inquiry about coach certification became the foundation for a leadership approach that has helped shape a thriving organization and a meaningful legacy.

The pages that follow are a reflection of that journey. They are not merely the observations of a successful financial advisor or business leader. They are the insights of a thoughtful practitioner who has spent years learning, listening, serving, leading, and growing alongside clients, colleagues, and communities. Ben writes from experience, but more importantly, he writes from conviction.

This book reflects the same values that have guided his life and leadership: integrity, trust, stewardship, continuous learning, and a genuine commitment to helping others flourish. Whether you are a leader, entrepreneur, advisor, coach, or someone seeking greater clarity and purpose in your own journey, you will find wisdom, practical insight, and meaningful reflection within these pages.

As I reflect on Ben's leadership and contribution, I am reminded that great leaders build successful organizations, but exceptional leaders build successful people who create exceptional organizations. Ben Russell is one of those leaders, and this book is a generous extension of that legacy.

I invite you to read with curiosity, reflect with intention, and consider how the ideas contained in these pages might influence your own leadership, decisions, and future.

*Dr. Shayne Tracy Founder,*

*International Institute of Coaching Practice (IICP) Originator, Sweet Spot™ Leadership and Coaching Framework*

## INTRODUCTION

# THE SOLO PRACTITIONER'S PARADOX

I WAS MORE SUCCESSFUL than I'd ever imagined.

And I was miserable.

Two hundred and fifty families trusted me with their life savings. My revenue exceeded anything I'd dreamed about when I started this business. Other advisors looked at my practice and saw exactly what they were working toward.

But I couldn't remember the last time I'd taken a full week off.

My calendar was booked solid for months. Client meetings stacked back-to-back, all of them necessary, all of them important. My family got whatever energy I had left at the end of the day, which wasn't much.

Sound familiar?

Maybe you're managing 200, 250, maybe 300 client relationships. You're making more money than you ever thought possible. Other advisors ask how you built such a great practice.

But you're exhausted.

You're missing family events. Your spouse is frustrated with your schedule. You can't remember the last time you felt genuinely excited about going to work.

And the thought of doing this for another ten or twenty years? You honestly don't know if you can.

This is the solo practitioner's paradox. Your success has become your trap.

## HOW WE GOT HERE

About fifteen years ago, I encountered Simon Sinek's work during a coaching certification through the International Behavioral Coaching Institute. He was exploring what consumers want, why people are inspired to take action, and how to build companies that last.

He introduced the concept of the infinite game. To me, this meant a business that can sustain itself beyond any one individual but still feels like a family firm.

This struck me. Why was everyone so focused on being the biggest rather than being the best?

Particularly in the finance industry, everything is about growth metrics and revenue targets and where you rank on the leaderboard.

There's a fundamental difference between business books that talk about how to grow a great business to make a ton of money and what Sinek was proposing, which was playing the infinite game based on values and guiding principles that serve people for decades to come.

Maybe it was because of my master's degree in wellness management and thinking about organizational health. Maybe it was because I'd always believed that if you did the right things for the right reasons, the results would follow.

Sinek's framework gave me permission to build a practice that wasn't about winning but about lasting.

This isn't another practice management book focused on metrics and growth charts. Instead, we're going to discuss building something that outlasts you and doing it in a manner that is in alignment with your values and culture.

## THERE'S ANOTHER WAY

I'm writing this book because I decided to take a different path.

That path was to build an infinite team of my own.

It isn't an easier path. Building an infinite team has been, and continues to be, the hardest thing I've done in my career. Harder than starting from scratch.

But it is giving me my life back.

And it is creating something that will outlast my career. Something that can keep the promises I've made to families who trust us with their futures.

I've spent twenty-five years building our financial advisory practice from the ground up, from solo practitioner to multi-advisor firm. My work as a Certified Behavioral Coach helped me understand the people side of this transition, which is honestly the hardest part.

## HERE'S WHAT WE'LL COVER

In the first few chapters, we'll look at the hidden costs of solo success that show up in unexpected places. We'll explore why discovering your purpose matters before building anything else and what makes a team infinite versus just bigger.

Then we'll get into the self-assessment. Are you built to lead a team? How do you know if joining makes more sense than building? These aren't easy questions, but they're essential.

If you decide to build, we'll walk through creating your team's foundation from values, not organizational charts. How to develop your advisor bench through the entire pipeline. The upstream activities that lead to sustainable growth.

We'll cover how to protect client relationships through change. You've spent years building trust with these families, and the last thing you want to do is break it. How to build a multi-generational practice that serves families across decades. What the seventy-five-year promise means and how it changes everything.

We'll explore how specialization works in a team environment and when joining beats building. If you're evaluating team opportunities, we'll look at what to look for and what red flags to avoid.

And we'll talk about finding balance in building something infinite. What becomes possible when you stop trying to do everything yourself? How to enjoy the ride while building something that outlasts your career.

## WHAT YOU NEED TO KNOW UP FRONT

This isn't a one-size-fits-all formula. What worked for us might not work exactly the same way for you.

I'm still on this journey. The process takes time. We spent a year just to develop our values and guiding principles. We invested years building our advisor bench before we could really start transitioning clients. It gets complicated before it gets easier.

And it requires letting go.

Letting go of being the smartest person in the room. Letting go of control. Letting go of your need to be the one who gets credit.

That's harder than any of the systems or structures.

Building with purpose, building from the inside out, building something designed to outlast your career is possible.

It's hard.

And it's worth it.

## LET'S START

Before we talk about how to build a team, we need to understand why most successful advisors even need one in the first place.

What are the hidden costs of success that show up in ways you might not even realize? How do you know when you've hit capacity? What are the warning signs? These are the ones you see and the ones you don't.

When my practice reached 250 families, I thought I had made it.

I had no idea what I was about to discover about the real price of that success.

## CHAPTER 1

# THE HIDDEN COSTS OF SUCCESS

WHEN MY PRACTICE HIT 250 families, I began to feel the pressure. As I rounded 275, I began to feel the pain. I saw 300 in the near future, and it began to stress me out. I needed to make a change. My calendar stopped being mine.

It belonged to the meetings. An endless stream of them, all necessary, all important, all demanding my time.

With a client list this size, you have to juggle a lot. Younger clients just starting their careers need one kind of guidance. Business owners with complex compensation and equity structures need something entirely different. Families approaching retirement, clients navigating end-of-life planning . . . each group deserves specialized attention, deep expertise, and real focus.

You become a mile wide and an inch deep.

You're trying to be an expert in equity compensation for your achievers, business valuations for your entrepreneurs, retirement planning for pre-retirees, Medicare and long-term care for retirees, and estate planning for your high-net-worth families.

That's five different specialties. Each one could be a full-time focus. But you're supposed to be great at all of them.

It's just not possible.

You get pretty good at the basics. But when a client has a truly complex issue, the kind that needs deep expertise, you're not able to serve them at the level they deserve.

I noticed that weeks turned into months of being over-worked. I was more stressed and enjoyed my job less and less. I became more irritable. I wasn't as excited to show up to work. I didn't have as much energy for my family.

In this chapter, let's explore the hidden costs of success as a solo practitioner. Some you're probably aware of. Others are showing up in ways you might not even realize.

## ONE PERSON CAN'T DO IT ALL

Most solo practitioners won't admit that, at a certain point, you hit a ceiling on service quality.

Is it because you stop working hard? No. You're probably working harder than ever.

Is it because your systems aren't good? No. You've likely built excellent processes over the years.

You hit the ceiling because one person simply cannot be all things to all people.

I'm not sure to what degree my clients observed the effect on quality. We worked extremely hard. We had very clean systems to maintain a high degree of quality. But they definitely felt that we were stretched thin. They felt that we were not taking on new clients. They wanted us to help their children, and we were hesitant because we didn't have the time.

So we had to make decisions. Which clients would we see once a year versus twice a year? We'd meet with their attorneys and CPAs if requested, but we didn't have time to proactively coordinate those relationships the way we should have.

A solo practitioner simply can't match that level of specialization. Even with a support staff. I couldn't, no matter how hard I tried.

## WARNING SIGNS

So how do you know you've hit capacity?

Sometimes it's obvious. You're exhausted, your family is frustrated, and your schedule is insane.

But more often it sneaks up on you.

You've probably heard of the boiling frog. Put a frog in water that's slowly heating up, and it doesn't jump out. The change is so gradual that it just normalizes the rising temperature. By the time it realizes what's happening, it's too late.

That's what capacity limits look like for most advisors. You say yes to one more client, then another. One hundred becomes 150. Then 200. Then 250. Then 300. And somewhere along the way, you stopped noticing the temperature rising because busy became your normal.

Here are the visible signs:

- You're tired and overwhelmed, consistently;
- Your family is frustrated with your schedule;
- Your team members are frustrated with your lack of availability to lead them;
- You may lose a few of your top clients because they haven't gotten the attention they deserve;
- You may lose a team member or a younger advisor, resulting in higher turnover, because you don't have time to lead your people;
- You're short-tempered with people around you.

A warning sign that should raise a red flag comes when you *ask your clients if they think you're taking on new relationships.*

As we built our team and went from two advisors to five, we went back to our client families and told them we were happy to help other friends and family members. I was shocked, genuinely shocked, at how many people said they didn't think I was taking on clients.

I wondered, "*What had I done to give them that impression?"- Done* I was not even aware that I was coming across as overworked and overwhelmed. Certainly not in front of clients. Many overworked advisors have no idea they're projecting capacity constraints.

One client told me, "You're like a secret Vermont lake I discovered. I don't want to share it because it's so special. I want to keep it to myself and make sure it stays that way."

Your best clients, the ones who love working with you, aren't referring their loved ones to you. Not because they don't want to help their friends and family but because they're afraid their referrals will dilute the attention they receive. They're protecting their own relationship with you by keeping quiet about how great you are.

So what happened when we built capacity?

## WHEN WE WENT BACK TO OUR CLIENTS

After we built our team, we went back to our clients and told them we were wide open for business. Happy to help.

Referral rates improved significantly, in some cases doubling, as clients understood the team had capacity to serve their family members.

We shared our mantra. *Invested in Family.*

We shared that the team was able to serve family members across the country. They quickly referred all their children. They began to refer more coworkers and friends. They trusted that if they referred someone, it wouldn't affect their own client service. Referral by referral, the practice grew.

## SO, WHERE DOES THIS LEAVE YOU?

If you're recognizing yourself in this chapter, you're probably asking, "Is there another way? Can I build something sustainable without sacrificing either my clients or my life?"

The answer is yes.

But it requires rethinking some fundamental assumptions about how an advisory practice operates and what success looks like.

Really, it starts with getting clear on why you do what you do. What's driving you? What matters most? Because before you can build something different, you need to understand what you're building toward.

In the next chapter, we'll explore those deeper motivations and values. The "how" of building a team matters. But the "why"? That matters more.

CHAPTER 2

# STARTING WITH WHY: DISCOVERING YOUR PURPOSE-DRIVEN PRACTICE

ONCE YOU REALIZE YOU need to build something beyond a solo practice, the question becomes, "Where do you start?"

Most advisors jump straight to the mechanics. How many people do I hire? What positions? How do I structure compensation? What systems do I need?

Those questions matter. But if you start there, you're building on sand.

So where should you start? I found the answer in an unexpected place. The answer was in Simon Sinek's concept of ***the infinite game.***

Even the consultants and coaches are wrapped up in the numbers. The charts. The spreadsheets. The analytics. Why was everyone so focused on being the biggest rather than being the best? In the financial world, there is always a given assumption that bigger is better. Consultants want to help you grow your business two or three times over. Our "why" was about building a team that was infinite and could serve generations of families. The growth is a result of doing that great work.

What would it look like to build a practice that wasn't about winning, but about lasting?

That question led us to do something that most advisors skip entirely. We built from the inside out.

## TWO PATHS FORWARD

There are really only two paths forward from here.

**Track One: Build your own values-based team.** You develop your values, hire people who align with them, build the infrastructure, and create the culture. You're the architect.

**Track Two: Join an existing values-based team.** You find a practice already built on strong values and become part of what they're creating.

The question is, *"Which one fits you?"*

Both tracks are fundamentally different from what most advisors are doing right now.

Most advisors are running what I call a **Lifestyle Practice**. And from here on out, that's the term I'm going to use instead of "solo practice," because that's really what we're talking about.

A Lifestyle Practice isn't just a one-person show. I know $4 million to $5 million teams that, under the hood, are really three rock stars running Lifestyle Practices under one roof. They may think they have all their ducks in a row. They've got buy-sell agreements. They've got succession plans on paper.

But ask one partner if they could handle their colleague's practice if that person didn't wake up tomorrow. They'd tell you, "Hell no. I'm already seeing thirty meetings a week, myself."

That's a Lifestyle Practice. Doesn't matter if it's one person or five. If it would all fall apart without you, if you're building something to eventually sell and take your chips off the table, if your clients' futures depend entirely on you staying healthy and engaged . . . that's a Lifestyle Practice.

There's nothing inherently wrong with that choice. But let's be honest about what it is.

The Lifestyle Practice is about building something that serves you during your career. The infinite team, what some call the enterprise model, means building something that outlasts your career and is focused on something greater.

So as you're thinking about your values and your why, ask yourself, "What am I building here?"

If you're building an infinite team, either track can work. Build it yourself or join one already established.

But if you're choosing the Lifestyle Practice model, be clear-eyed about what that means for your clients. What happens to them when you're gone? Are they served as well? The rest of this book is written for people choosing the infinite team path. Whether you're on Track One or Track Two, the principles are the same. The values work matters. The team structure matters. The multigenerational thinking matters.

If you're reading this and realizing you're more suited to the Lifestyle Practice model? That's okay. That's part of the process of figuring out your why. Better to know that now.

## WHEN YOUR TEAM WANTS THIS

Now, you might be wondering, didn't anyone push back on this? Didn't your partners think this was soft stuff that wouldn't move the needle?

Originally, the team felt the pressure of growth as we were understaffed from an advisor standpoint, but we were fortunate to have a great culture. As the saying goes, "Nothing changes if nothing changes." Once the team realized that we had to evolve and grow, we asked them, "So now that we realize that we must double in size over time to serve generations of families, what makes us special? What cultural norms, values, and guiding principles make us, *us*? The us that we don't want to lose as we grow? Who would like to be a part of a team-building process to refine our values and create guiding principles so that we are more clear with who we are, so we know our cultural roots as we grow?"

As the branches of our trees grow, our roots grow deeper. As the team understood this, everyone wanted to be a part of the process of refining and defining our culture.

With only two equity shareholders and partners at the time, it was really up to the two of us to decide if we were okay with focusing on purpose over immediate profit metrics. We believed that by focusing on the people and the service, the profits would follow as long as we ran a smart, efficient business.

And that's how our journey started.

But I recognize we were fortunate. Many advisors face real resistance when they bring up values and purpose. Partners who think it's a waste of time, team members who just want to know their compensation structure, and the pressure to focus on the numbers because that's what the industry measures.

If you're facing that resistance, you may need to start smaller. Get clear on your own "why" first, then bring others along gradually. Or it might mean the people around you aren't aligned with where you want to go.

## THE YEAR-LONG JOURNEY

We weren't just going to hang values on the wall and move on. We were going to figure out who we were before we decided what we were going to build.

We went through a year-long process of trying to capture the nuggets within our culture that made us great.

We started by asking the team some questions:

- *When we double in size, what are the things we have today that we don't want to lose?*
- *As we serve our families, what makes us great? What makes us special? What makes us different?*
- *As we work with each other, what messages do we want to give ourselves to remind us of the journey we're on?*

We did a tremendous amount of research. We reviewed values, guiding principles, and missions from different companies. We met monthly to consider many phrases, values, and quotes as potential company guiding principles.

Really, it was a list of more than 200 words and phrases. We all spent two months researching guiding principles and values, and then we threw this whole mess together. It left us asking, "How are we going to come up with anything coherent from this?"

I told my team, "It's going to be a long process, but it's going to be fun. I think we will be able to find five to seven values, and five to ten guiding principles." According to my research, that tends to be where companies that do this work often land.

We first sifted through those hundreds of words and refined them down to a short list of fifty to seventy-five quotes, phrases, and values.

Then we did another round of exercises where we cast anonymous votes to see which ones resonated most with the team. We had deep discussions about these values and principles. What would they mean to our team? More importantly, what would they mean to our clients?

We allowed team members to advocate for the phrases and values they found most meaningful.

And then six principles and phrases appeared in everyone's top ten.

In the end, we agreed on three core values, three cultural values, and seven guiding principles.

Then we lived with them. After about a year and a half, we dropped one guiding principle that simply wasn't being used. And that's okay. That's part of the process. It's better to acknowledge what's not working than to keep it on the wall because we spent time on it.

**CREATIVE PROCESS TRANSFORMATION**

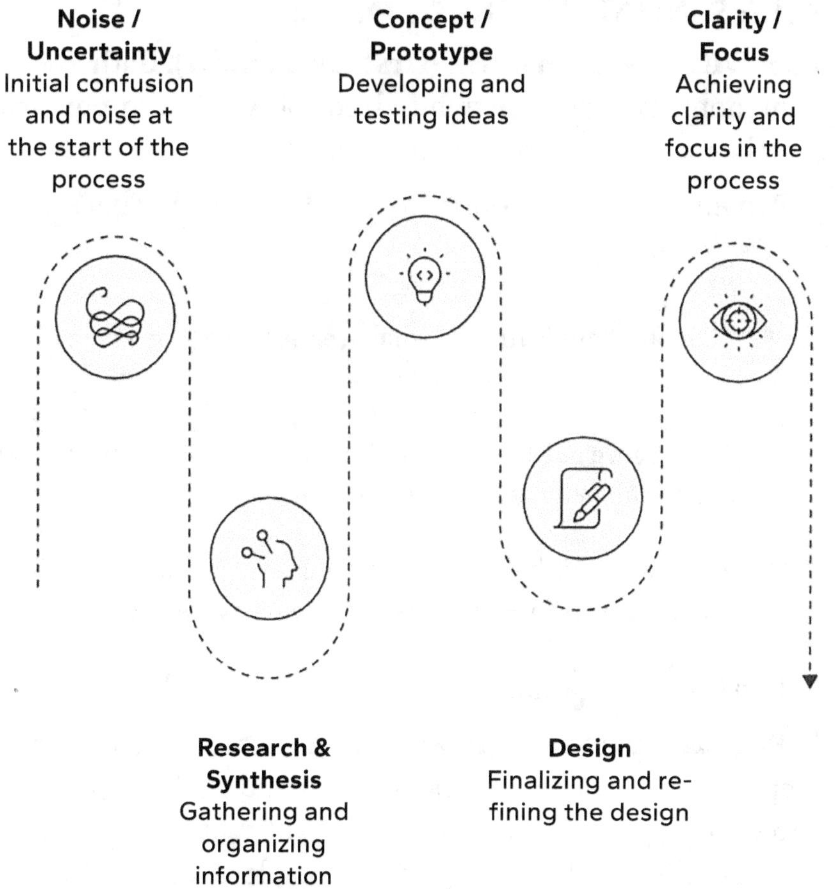

## HOW TO FIND YOUR GUIDING PRINCIPLES

So what did we learn from that year-long journey?

Let me walk you through the process. But first, understand this isn't a weekend retreat exercise. This takes time. When you involve your entire team in the process, you create something that everyone owns. Something that will guide your decisions when things get tough.

## HERE'S WHAT WORKED FOR US:

**Start with the brainstorm (first few months).** Gather your team monthly. Brainstorm hundreds of words and phrases. Let it be messy. It's supposed to be messy.

Remember the questions we asked our team? That's your starting point.

- When we double in size, what are the things we have today that we don't want to lose?
- As we serve our families, what makes us great? What makes us special? What makes us different?
- As we work with each other, what messages do we want to give ourselves to remind us of the journey we're on?

Don't try to organize yet. Just capture everything.

**Find the patterns (next few months).** What themes keep emerging? What shows up again and again? Put words into grouping categories. Be clear about what you're trying to accomplish. Values? Guiding principles? Mission? All of the above?

What happens if you skip this step and jump straight to voting? You don't want to commit to anything too soon. Let the process play out.

**Narrow it down (months later).** Go through multiple rounds of refining. Use anonymous voting. You want to know what people *really* believe, not what they think you want to hear. Have discussions. Let people advocate for what matters to them.

This is where the real work happens. You're not just picking words. You're discovering what you believe as a team. What are you willing to make hard decisions around? What will you defend even when it's inconvenient?

**Live with it (the next year).** With your guiding principles and values outlined, revisit your mission and vision. You might need to make substantial adjustments. Then live your values over the next year. See what gets used. See what guides real decisions. See what sits on the wall, ignored.

Trust the process.

**Refine and commit (year two and beyond).** Test that your mission aligns with your values. Drop anything that isn't working. Double down on what is.

The goal isn't perfection. The goal is clarity about who you are and what you stand for.

**What mistakes should you avoid?** Don't do this as just the partners or owners. Involve the whole team. Don't try to rush the timeline. Don't hang values on the wall and think you're done. And whatever you do, don't skip the messy brainstorming phase. The mess is where the good stuff lives.

## WHAT IF YOU'RE SOLO RIGHT NOW?

Now, I recognize not everyone reading this has a team to involve in a year-long process. Maybe you're a solo practitioner trying to figure out your next move. Maybe you have one assistant and you're wondering if this even applies to you.

It does. You just start differently.

You can begin with these questions for yourself:

- What drew me to this work in the first place before the metrics and the growth targets?
- What do my best clients say they value most about working with me? Not what you think they value? What do they tell you?
- If I could only do three things for clients, what would matter most? What would you refuse to give up, even if someone offered you more money to do something else?
- What would I refuse to compromise on, even if it costs me revenue? Where's your line?
- When I imagine my practice in ten years, what do I want to be true about it beyond the financials?

Get clarity for yourself first. Write it down. Live with it for a few months. See if it holds up when you make actual decisions.

Once you have that clarity, you can bring others into the conversation, whether that's your first hire or a group of advisors you're considering joining.

The process I described above? You can adapt it. Start with your own brainstorm. Talk to your best clients, and ask them what they value. Look for patterns in what you naturally gravitate toward. Then, when you do bring someone onto your team, you'll have a foundation to build from rather than trying to figure it out together from scratch.

## WHEN YOUR WHY FINDS YOU

Years ago, we hired a branding and marketing firm. They were observing how we talked about our work, and they picked up on something we hadn't even noticed.

We kept using the word "families" instead of "clients."

It wasn't intentional. It was just how we naturally thought about the people we served.

The marketing firm helped us turn that observation into our mantra of Invested in Family. They took a term from our industry, "invested," and used it in a creative way. We aren't just investing money. We're investing in families.

At first, that's all it was. A mantra.

But several years later, as we built our team, we realized there was more to it. The phrase kept showing up in how we made decisions. So we expanded the definition into three prongs.

First, we serve our client families. That's the foundation.

Second, we are committed to our team members and think of each other as family. If we're building something that lasts, the people building it need to belong.

Third, being part of a growing firm allows our team members to achieve career goals, which allows them to help their own individual families. How misaligned would it be if we're helping our client families achieve their dreams while our team members can't achieve dreams for their own families?

And then we added the seventy-five-year promise, which is our commitment that our firm will serve our client families for life and be a firm where our youngest team members can have thriving careers until their retirement, long after I'm gone.

All together, *our team is an infinite team that is Invested in Family for life.*

That's our why.

It didn't come from a weekend retreat. It evolved from paying attention to how we naturally operated, then getting intentional about it.

Your why might work the same way. Pay attention to the patterns in how you talk about your work, the decisions you make, what your best clients say they value. Your why might already be there. You just need to notice it.

## WHEN VALUES CHANGE YOUR MISSION

So we had our values. That should have been the end of it. But we didn't expect that clarifying our values exposed a gap in our mission. We realized our mission statement didn't match what we believed. So, we added one word. *Generations.*

As we gained clarity on our values, we had to refine our mission statement. Our mission became, ***"We help generations of families make educated financial decisions, so they are more confident about their future."***

The phrase "generations of families" represents a major change. We were committing to a multigenerational approach, and that our team will be able to serve my seventy-five-year-old client, their fifty-year-old child, and their twenty-five-year-old grandchild for life (what we call the seventy-five-year promise).

When you make a seventy-five-year promise to families and put that at the center of what you do, it makes it extremely clear that you must create an infinite team. That timeline is simply beyond one person's career.

What kind of team do you need to keep a seventy-five-year promise? What kind of advisors do you need to develop? How do you ensure the culture survives beyond the founders?

These questions led us down a completely different hiring path.

## HOW VALUES WORK WHEN THE STAKES ARE HIGH

You might be wondering, *"Okay, but how do values help when you're making hard decisions?"*

When you take your time developing guiding principles and values and when the entire team is brought into the process, it gives you clarity when things get messy.

A phrase I heard at a recent conference that changed how I think about leadership is, **"The goal as a leader is to make the intangible tangible."**

Team dynamics, client relationships, culture, and trust are all intangible things. But when you're having a difficult dialogue with a team member, a guiding principle or value can make something more concrete. It gives you a marker or reference point to check whether your actions and behaviors are aligned with your values.

For example, one of our guiding principles is ***Start Where You Are.***

When a client says, "How can you help me? Maybe I should be further ahead," it's a lot easier to say, "We have a guiding principle to *start where you are*. That's our planning process."

The principle guides how we talk to clients. It guides how we talk to each other. It guides who we serve and how we serve them.

What happens when two team members disagree and both think they're right? You go back to the values. If we think about our core value of service, what would we do? If we think about our cultural value of sustainability, what would we do? The members of our team are wired to provide white-glove service to everyone. They love to help. They care. It is a wonderful part of our culture. But at times, we have to ask ourselves, "If we do this for one client, could we do it for all clients? Could we do it for all platinum clients? All gold clients? All silver clients? Is it sustainable?"

In Patrick Lencioni's Five Behaviors of a Cohesive Team model, he talks about healthy conflict. Conflict on a team is normal, and a great way to lean into healthy conflict is to engage in dialogue that is less about the difference of opinion between two people and more about whether the "thing" we are discussing is in alignment or misalignment with our values and guiding principles.

**PYRAMID OF TEAM DYNAMICS**

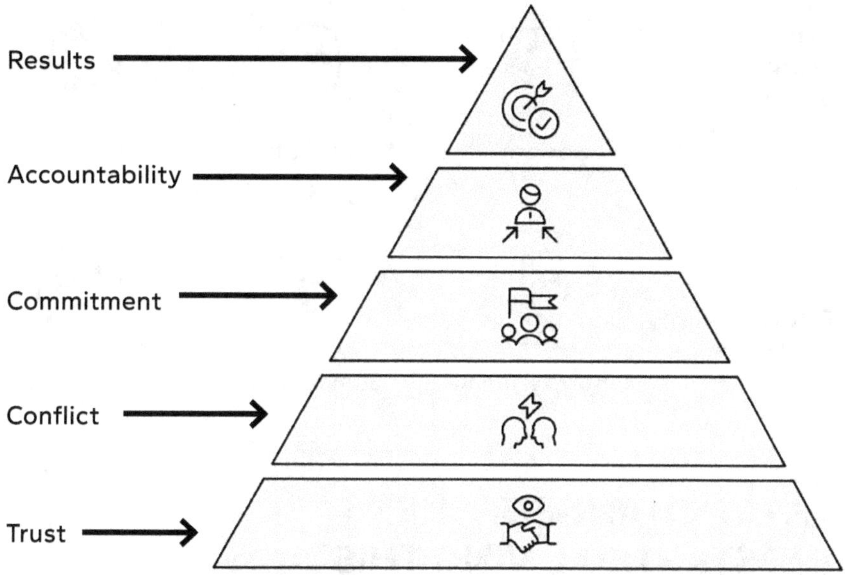


Larger teams are complex. You've got to build systems. You've got to get systems out of your head and onto paper, so other people can follow them. You've got to have multiple meetings to get everyone rowing in the same direction.

It gets complicated. You're dealing with different variables, your people are dealing with new systems, and it's clunky.

You're constantly searching for simplicity on the far side of complexity. Things start simple. As they grow, they become complex. But there's the possibility of getting to the other side of that complexity to find simplicity again.

## VALUES

| | | | |
|---|---|---|---|
| OUR CORE VALUES | Service | Integrity | Teamwork |
| OUR CULTURAL VALUES | Empowerment | Commitment | Sustainability |

## WHAT CHANGED WHEN WE STARTED LIVING THIS

So what happened when we started living these values?

- We gained clarity on the types of clients we serve and where to draw the line, like what level of net worth or complexity a client must have for us to work with them effectively. Sometimes this simply means we delay a formal client relationship until a later stage in their life;
- We got laser-focused on the right financial planning costs and services;
- We understood that parents want to help their kids get the financial education they need to get ahead. So we created options. A parent could pay for their adult child's ongoing financial planning. It wasn't a huge expense for the parents, but it gave their thirty-year-old the guidance they needed when making critical early-career financial decisions;

- We began taking on more clients as we told our families we were happy to help family members throughout the country. In fact, we doubled our number of referrals and doubled our number of new clients per year. When clients understood our purpose of serving generations of families, they wanted to bring their family members in. They trusted we'd take care of the people they love.

Our team members became more excited to help generations of families because they knew that was our purpose. In the past, an older client or a younger client without significant assets might get ignored or pushed aside. A team member might be annoyed to work with a client with so few assets.

But today? When your team understands the "why" behind serving a thirty-year-old with limited assets, it's not a burden. It's an investment in a relationship that could span generations. But in order to meet our value of sustainability, we needed to align the costs and services provided.

## THE ONGOING JOURNEY

Now, you might be thinking this sounds like a lot of work for something that might not stick. What I can say confidently is that the process itself is worth it.

I'm absolutely still on this journey. How do I talk less and ask more great questions? How do we keep these values alive as we grow? How do we make sure new team members really understand what we're about? What happens when team members understand they're building something that outlasts them?

These aren't questions you answer once. They're questions you keep asking.

There's a concept from George Leonard's book *Mastery* that says the master's journey is 90 percent calm waters, punctuated by intense periods of growth. You prepare yourself. You take a leap. You're hanging on for dear life, but you're also having fun. Then you regroup at that next level, build systems, and breathe for a bit before the next leap.

Building with purpose follows the same pattern. You'll have periods of stability where your values guide you. Then you'll face growth that tests whether those values can scale. You'll wonder if you made the right choices. You'll refine. You'll drop what isn't working. And then you'll find simplicity on the far side of complexity.

But when you have that clarity, when your team knows what you stand for, the hard decisions get clearer. Not easier necessarily but clearer.

You can't build an infinite team without this foundation. You can hire people, create org charts and implement systems. But without shared values and a clear purpose, you're just building a bigger version of the same thing.

The Lifestyle Practice problem doesn't get solved by adding more people. It gets solved by building something bigger than any one person, something worth sustaining beyond your own career.

When we hired a marketing firm, one of their tasks was helping us find a name for the company. It is a surprisingly difficult process. Most meaningful words are already taken. The consultant explained that the best company names rarely mean anything at first. Think about names like Apple or Google. Before those companies existed, those words had nothing to do with technology. The meaning was built over time through the work, the service, and the culture behind them. He told us that whatever name we chose, it would feel empty at the start, but if we built something worth believing in, the name would eventually carry the weight of everything we stood for. Today, that is exactly what happened. Our name has tremendous meaning in my heart and mind. It represents the entity that ensures our team members have great careers, our clients are served, and they can achieve their goals.

This was evidenced when we recently received branded clothing, everyone was more proud of wearing company branded gear than they ever were wearing the names of the partners (our old firm's name). We have created an entity that has a different meaning and greater purpose.

What we built has tremendous meaning in my heart and mind. Our company is not just a business. It is the entity that ensures our team members have great careers, our clients are served, and they can achieve their goals. As a leader, my job is to care for this company because this company cares for all of us. My hope is that all members of our team believe they are working for something greater than any individual, for a purpose that outlasts all of us, versus working for a boss.

That starts with knowing your why.

Once you have that foundation, once you know what you stand for and what you're building toward, you can begin to envision what an infinite team looks like. Not just more people doing more things, but a fundamentally different structure built to outlast any single person's career.

And that's where we're headed next.

CHAPTER 3

# THE INFINITE TEAM FRAMEWORK: BEYOND THE LIFESTYLE PRACTICE

ORIGINALLY, WE HAD A great team supporting three solo practitioners. On paper, it looked like we'd figured it out. We had systems, we had people, and we were serving clients well.

Underneath it all, team members were essentially working for three different bosses who sometimes disagreed or wanted things done "their way." We each had our own client relationships, our own way of doing things, and our own vision for the future.

We'd built something successful. But was it what we wanted to build? Was it what the clients needed?

That's when I had to ask myself a harder question. *What am I building toward?*

Most advisors I talk to land in one of two camps:

- They're building a lifestyle practice. A great business designed to fund their retirement and then sell to the highest bidder;
- They're building an infinite team. A practice designed to outlast any single career.

Both are legitimate choices. But they're fundamentally different.

You can't build an infinite team by accident. You have to choose it. You have to understand what you're signing up for and why it matters enough to take on the complexity.

In this chapter, we'll explore what separates lifestyle practices from infinite teams, what makes a team truly infinite, and how to know if this path is right for you. We'll look at the before-and-after of what changes when you make this transition.

## THE LIFESTYLE PRACTICE VS. THE INFINITE TEAM

Let me be clear. I'm not here to judge lifestyle practices.

In our industry, lifestyle practices serve clients well and have tremendous value. A well-organized solo practitioner can build an excellent business, serve clients beautifully, and sell it to a competent team at the end of their career. Their clients will be well served, even if the business name and the people change.

But a lifestyle practice starts and ends with the career of one person. An infinite team is built to live beyond any one person.

So what does that mean?

A lifestyle practice might sell to a larger team in a different state. Maybe that team keeps one local advisor and eliminates part of the staff due to redundancy. Maybe some of your legacy clients get turned into the home office 1-800 call center. Most clients still get served but not all. Most team members will keep their jobs but not all.

An infinite team means that your team's careers are not bound to a partner's retirement. You're building something that creates opportunity for everyone. Just as the service of your families is infinite, so is the demand for the great work of your team.

When I did some serious soul-searching about this choice, I kept coming back to one thing. How could the journey be self-serving when families wanted us to help their children, and we wanted to create opportunities for younger advisors? How could any of that be time-bound to my retirement? I realized the second half of my career needed to be focused on serving others (clients and team members).

So let's talk about what it takes to build something infinite.

## WHAT MAKES A TEAM TRULY INFINITE?

Let's go back to Simon Sinek and start with why.

### THE WHY

An infinite team has a mission, a mantra, and values and guiding principles so deeply embedded in the culture that generations of people are inspired to continue that purpose.

As we reflected on the definition of *Invested in Family*, it became very clear that we must create an infinite team. Not "should." Not "maybe someday." But "must"! It was the only option.

But having a compelling why isn't enough. You need the people to carry it forward.

## THE WHO

Multiple shareholders, multiple advisors, multiple supporting team members of different ages. So that as one team member retires, another one is ready to grow into that opportunity.

I never understood internship programs. There was too much of a lift to have an unskilled person work with us for ten weeks and jump through all of the hiring requirements in the finance industry. But when you understand more about building talent for an infinite team, you realize that this is the upstream activity that finds talent. On the next page is our diagram that outlines the talent pipeline. Creating an internship program sifts through talented college students who think that they are excited about this industry. After working with them for a few months, you know whether they'd be great team members. It's the upstream activity that builds the bench and ensures the infinite nature of the people on the team.

And then you need systems that outlast any individual person.

**INFINITE TEAM MODEL**

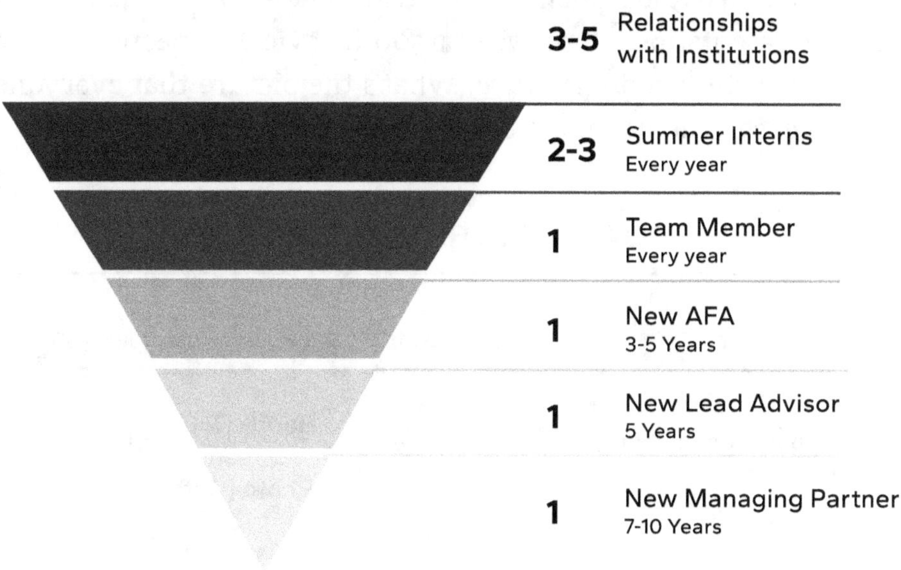


## THE HOW

The repeatable systems that create a consistent client experience. In this industry, we know that when we create a system, it works 93 percent of the time. There will always be exceptions.

We believe in kaizen or continuous improvement. No system is ever finished, but a system gives us the ability to make the intangible tangible. To hang our hat on something very specific that we can repeat. We repeat these systematic activities, and they become habits. It starts to feel like it does when you brush your teeth. Do your systems depend on you, or are they repeatable by others? Can other people on your team teach new team members those systems? If you answered yes to both of these questions, you are getting in the ballpark.

One of our core values is sustainability. So every system must be repeatable and sustainable.

We use tools such as our "team maps," which are visual representations that give us a 500-foot view, so people can see the system and structure. What's the picture that everyone needs in their mind to row in the same direction?

**ROWING IN THE SAME DIRECTION**

| ANNUAL | | | | |
|---|---|---|---|---|
| Team Lunch (Jan) | Happy Hour (April) | Summer Event & Volunteer (July) | Happy Hour & Team Photo (Oct) | Pie Event (Nov) |

| BI-ANNUAL | | | |
|---|---|---|---|
| Business Planning (1d MST Jul / 2d offsite Dec) | Achievement Reviews (Jan & July) | Sarah & Molly Mtg (1 wk before breakfast) | CBC Breakfast (July & Dec) |

| QUARTERLY | | |
|---|---|---|
| Marblestone Mtg – 4 hrs (Jan/Apr/Jul/Oct) | Leadership Mtgs – 3 hrs (Jan/Apr/Jul/Oct) | Partner Meeting – 2 hrs |

| MONTHLY | | |
|---|---|---|
| Touchstone Meeting – 2 hrs | Team 1:1's w/ Sarah – 60 min | Dan and Sarah 1:1 |

| BI-MONTHLY | |
|---|---|
| Advisor Training – 1 hr<br>*Jane join at ½ hour | Jack/Ally Investment<br>Mtg – 1 hr |

| WEEKLY | |
|---|---|
| Monday All Team Mtg – 1 hour | Leader Huddle – 45 min |

| DAILY |
|---|
| Team Meeting – 30 Minutes (Tuesday – Friday) |

We also map out when we meet, how often, and for what purpose. What's the sweet spot where we come together enough to stay aligned without "death by meetings"? This is important as teams grow from small to medium. You hit capacity limits and build in complexity.

## THE BIGGER PICTURE

There is also a business case to be made. Someone in a lifestyle practice reaches capacity sooner and struggles more to solve it because it's limited by one brain, one human, and the amount of time one person can work! The infinite team will have multiple brains around the table to look at the same situation in multiple ways.

The infinite team creates a C-suite. CEO, COO, CIO, and CFO, where leaders specialize and get better within their domains. No one person can do all of this well. This is the concept of 1+1+1=4. An infinite team creates something beyond the sum of its parts.

For the last thirty years, there's been enough margin in the finance industry that those in a lifestyle practice can thrive. But like any maturing industry, margins shrink as consumers expect more for less. Most advisors coming into this industry will join teams. Lifestyle practices will lose market share to elite teams, and they will be a smaller percentage of the industry. The economy of scale continues to climb, which will make it more difficult for lifestyle practices to get into business and stay in business.

I've been part of a team since 2003, when teaming wasn't popular. Today, highly effective teams are growing at a pace unfathomable to solo practitioners. The data is clear. It is no longer a debate.

So what does this look like in practice?

## WHAT ONLY AN INFINITE TEAM CAN DO

Only an infinite team can say to the eighty-five-year-old couple that they have advisors who focus on legacy, generational planning, long-term care needs, and estate planning; and say to their thirty-year-old grandchildren, having their first child, that they have advisors who focus on young achievers and families who need retirement planning and the protection of life insurance and disability; and have advisors who focus on business owners managing concentrated wealth or families transitioning to retirement with all the decisions around Social Security, pensions, and creating paychecks.

But it's not only that the infinite team has the ability to serve all these different types of families.

The advisors on the infinite team have the ability to choose. Each individual advisor is unique and gets more excited about different things. Over time, the team can focus more on specific topics and specialties that drive them. People who like working with older families can predominantly work with older families. People who like working with the younger generation can focus there.

Being a part of an elite team is a true win-win. The advisor can focus on the work they like to do with the families they like to work with. Clients get to work with a practitioner who is focused on their demographics and their needs. This also prevents the solo practitioner's challenge of becoming a generalist who is a mile wide and an inch deep. To be an expert at anything, you must be an inch wide and a mile deep.

## WHAT CHANGED: THE BEFORE AND AFTER

Prior to creating an infinite team, we had a really good team. It was an efficient lifestyle practice. I personally was feeling the capacity of my time, energy, and brain power. I was trying to serve all clients at all stages. Year by year, I became more of a generalist.

After the transition, I became laser-focused on the families that were most suited for me, and I was able to transition certain families to other advisors who were better suited to serve their needs. Because of this, I went from 225 clients to 100.

I have more energy, more passion, more ability to serve, and more brain power to specialize.

Before the conversion, the cracks showed up in small ways. A team member would follow one partner's process, only to have another partner redirect them. There was no single way of doing things because there was no single voice leading the practice.

With an infinite team, we were able to realign people to not just work with a specific advisor but with the whole team. There is a saying that you fall in love with the process, not the people. Of course, human capital is extremely important, but you want to make sure that the service isn't dependent on one person. If someone on the team says, "I want to do it my way," we might ask them, "What is the team's way?" We are all committed to being in alignment with the team way.

After the transition, we hear, "We're doing this because it's the infinite team system. It's in line with our core value of commitment. We are committed to following our team systems."

The entire ecosystem is different between a business that revolves around one person and a business that revolves around one purpose.

When done right, the people of an infinite team will have forgotten who the original partners were. All they know is that our company has a set of values and guiding principles that will sustain them in the long run, far beyond any of our lifetimes.

## HOW DO YOU KNOW IF IT'S WORKING?

So how do you measure success in this transition?

The real test of an infinite team isn't what happens when everything's running smoothly. It's what happens when you face disruption, like when an advisor retires or, worse, when something unexpected happens.

No matter the circumstance, your clients should experience equal or greater service during transitions. They're not panicking or asking to leave. They already know the other advisors on the team. The transition feels natural, not forced.

Team members maintain work-life balance during the change. They're not overwhelmed trying to absorb everything overnight.

The team continues to have capacity and room to grow. A partner's retirement creates opportunity rather than chaos. Research shows that elite teams strive to maintain a team that is at 80 percent capacity. This requires hiring and training before it is absolutely needed.

Clients are genuinely happy for the retiring advisor. Not just polite, but happy. Because they knew this was coming, and they trust the team will continue to serve them well.

Recently, we had an advisor who had a baby and stepped out of the workforce. We had conversations with seventy-five clients and transitioned them to other advisors. The advisors asked what they should tell clients. We said, "The truth." What a wonderful story that this advisor was stepping out of the workforce to be a stay-at-home parent, as their spouse had major demands at work. We assured the clients that our team was here to serve, and there would be no change to their investments, strategy, or client service. The clients were sad to see the advisor go, but they had no issues with the transition and completely understood. We didn't lose a single client. The clients had a deeper connection with our team. This unexpected advisor transition tested our values. Were we committed to these families? Were we available to serve them? Could we make adjustments, absorb these clients, and still enjoy the ride? Fortunately, the answer to these questions was yes!

## THE INFINITE INFANCY

I believe that we are still in the infinite infancy of an infinite team.

We might still hear team members comparing the way it used to be versus the way it is now when they are teaching interns. But there will be a day when that intern becomes a team member and teaches the next intern about our systems and our values, and they don't even remember the old way.

That is when we'll be at the next stage of the infinite team.

As a leader, I desire to create an environment that allows people to feel good. As much as I care about people, my job as a leader is to be loyal to our company and our clients first. This entity will live on to serve generations of families and generations of team families.

So where does this leave you?

If you're considering this path, the next question isn't about systems or org charts. It's more personal. We realize that these concepts may be a paradigm shift and that these are big changes that occur in an organization.

So, ask yourself, "Am I built to lead a team? Or am I better suited to be part of one?"

CHAPTER 4

# THE HONEST SELF-ASSESSMENT: ARE YOU BUILT TO LEAD A TEAM?

WHEN I STARTED THIS business, everything was about myself.

I positioned myself as the advisor who would help this family. I was on my own little island, dialing for dollars, busting my hump, beating the streets to find one client at a time. Then I'd try to convince that client I was competent enough to serve them.

The successful advisors achieve that goal. They take on client after client. As their client base grows, so does their confidence in themselves and, in some cases, their ego. The same self-centered perspective and overconfidence can get them stuck. They hit ceilings and capacity limitations and have to reinvent.

But there is an old adage: "What got you here won't get you there." The first phase of your successful career is about you; the next phase is about others. It is about moving from success to significance. It is larger than you. In this chapter, we'll explore the questions you need to ask yourself before deciding to build a team, how to recognize if you're better suited to joining rather than building, and the blind spots that trip up even the most successful advisors.

So let's start with the most important question: Are you built for this?

## THE HARD QUESTIONS

If you are considering building a team, here are some hard questions worth asking yourself:

- *What are the factors driving you to build a team?*
- *Do you have time or interest in recruiting and training the next generation of advisors?*
- *Can you let go of control as you transfer the bottom half of your practice to other advisors to give you the time to work ON the business?*
- *Are you willing to have your net income go down as you build out your team?*
- *Are you prepared to own a percent of something larger versus 100 percent of something smaller?*
- *Can you put the success of others ahead of your own?*
- *And are you prepared for the complexity of a team?*

The dedication you put toward growing your own practice was extremely hard but also completely within your control. Building an elite team will take five to ten times the amount of focus and energy as you weave through complexity and work with people to inspire them to become great advisors and stewards of what you've built.

Another question is, "*Do you enjoy being a leader?*"

Do you want to put in the time to sharpen the saw and become a great leader in the same way you spent years becoming a great advisor?

Do you find enjoyment in mentoring younger advisors and team members? Watching those team members have successful careers like you've had?

Can you put *we* before *I*?

## SEEING YOUR BLIND SPOTS

As you're working through those hard questions, there's something else worth considering: What are your blind spots?

I've noticed that the traits that make you successful in a lifestyle practice, such as being driven, competitive, and believing you can do it better than anyone else, can work against you as a leader.

Take motivation, for example.

If you're monetarily driven and competitive, you probably assume your team members are wired the same way. But the research shows that while people *do* want to be compensated fairly, they're more motivated by being appreciated, being part of a cohesive team, and doing great work.

So when you dangle a bigger bonus but push them too hard and then wonder why your team isn't as excited as you'd be? That's a blind spot.

And then there's delegation.

You probably believe you can do it better than others. And honestly? The results often prove you right. But leadership isn't about being the best at everything. It's about empowering others. Giving people the opportunity to learn, grow, and succeed. It took us fifteen to thirty years to get where we are today; it will take younger advisors time. However, with a team environment and some great mentoring and leadership, our hope is that what took us twenty years might only take ten for an associate advisor because they have mentors, a framework, and a process.

This success is not overnight. That's where the patience comes in . . . the kind of patience most successful advisors struggle with. So instead of developing people, you hold too much responsibility. Do too much. The business becomes you.

Ask yourself, *"If I didn't wake up tomorrow, would the business survive? Would it thrive?"*

Some advisors say, "Yes, I have a buy-sell agreement. Other advisors will step in to serve my clients."

But then I think about these questions:

- What happens to the culture of a company when it's bought by a different company?
- What happens to the client experience?
- What happens to the rest of the team where there may be redundancy?

## HOW TO EVALUATE YOURSELF

So, how do you evaluate yourself honestly?

There are plenty of assessments out there. DISC, StrengthsFinder, Kolbe, Working Genius. We use DISC with our team.

Much of our industry is high "S" and "C" on the DISC assessment. They're steady, systematic, and analytic. They follow systems. You tell them what to do, and they'll execute it perfectly.

I'm high "D" and "I," which is pretty different. "D" tendencies help you drive an agenda and lead people. "I" tendencies mean you care deeply about people over systems.

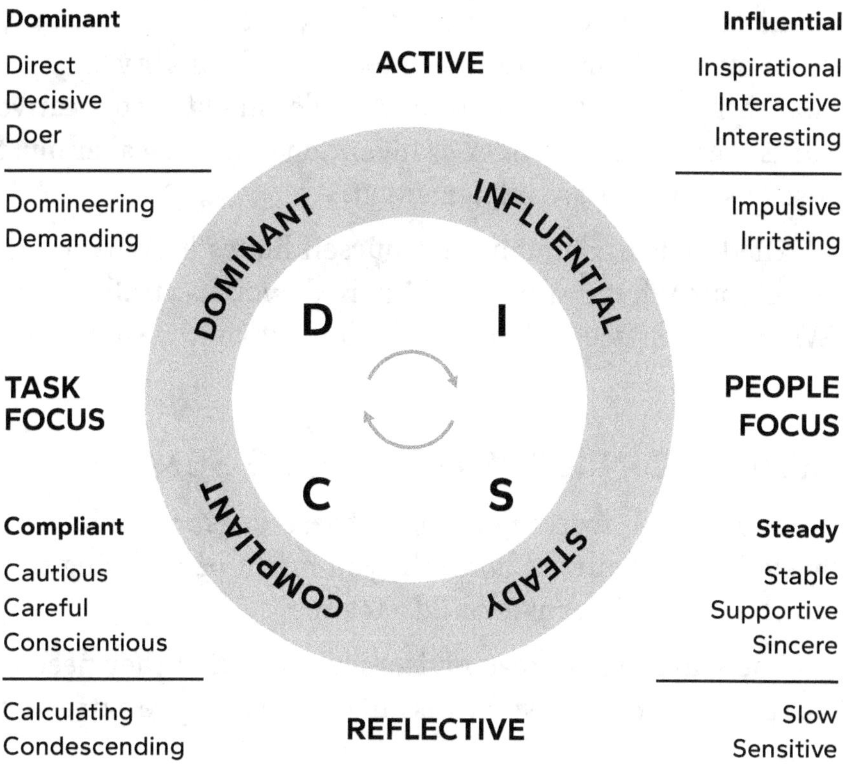

I'm not saying these are the tendencies a leader needs. But my preferences are very different from many other people in this industry. This is helpful because it's my job to see around the corner, leap when others aren't ready, lead into uncharted waters, and make the intangible tangible.

Understanding these differences has saved us from countless conflicts. When I want to leap, and my team wants to analyze, I know it's not resistance. It's their wiring asking good questions that my wiring would skip right over. One concept that has been invaluable for me is to move slower to grow faster. As leaders, we can guide the team to new heights, but only at the team's pace. The journey is no longer about what one person can do; it's about what a team can do.

*Working Genius* identifies the different characteristics that make teams effective at accomplishing their goals. Many team members are detail-oriented with the ability to organize things at the 100-foot level. A leader might need creative skills found in the Wonder or Invention traits. A leader must also ensure ideas are implemented.

The key is understanding yourself honestly. What energizes you? What drains you? Where do you naturally excel? Where do you need others to complement your weaknesses?

## WHEN JOINING MAKES MORE SENSE

Now, as you're working through these questions and really evaluating yourself honestly, you might be realizing that maybe you don't want to build a team.

There are many great advisors who do what they need to do so that they can have successful careers. They're extremely giving outside of work. They support their families, raise their children, volunteer, and give to charities.

If you see work as a means to your own end, and your career has been so successful that you don't have the work-life balance you desire, you might be a great fit for joining a team.

A team will allow you to continue being a successful advisor and have more balance in life.

I've had this conversation with dozens of advisors over the years. Like Robert,[1] who had 375 clients and couldn't see straight. When I asked him, "If you could wave a magic wand, what would you like to do?" His answer was immediate.

"I'd like to get the bottom half of my practice off my plate. I'd like to go down to my top fifty to onehundred clients and move up-market. I'm still hungry. I have talent. I've been in the business for twenty-five years. I can attract higher net worth people. But I need help."

That's exactly what a proven team can provide. A transition process over one to two years, where those base-level clients get excellent service from other advisors who specialize in serving families at that stage. And Robert can focus on what he does best.

The challenge? Robert felt he'd invested too much in his own systems and tools. He couldn't stomach the idea of adopting someone else's way of doing things. Maybe he'd have to change broker-dealers. He couldn't get over the hump.

So he stayed where he was, cobbling along, maintaining that level of stress and exhaustion. Last I heard, he's still there. Still successful by every external measure. Still exhausted. He made his choice. It just wasn't the choice that would give him his life back.

## IF YOU DECIDE TO BUILD

So if you've worked through these questions, if you've evaluated yourself honestly and you genuinely want to build, then the next question becomes, "What does this journey require?"

My personal journey began with a leadership class in grad school taught by my favorite professor, David Gobble. It continued through programs like Leadership Champlain. It deepened when I got my behavioral coaching certification through the International Behavioral Coaching Institute. I read books like *Tribe* and *Good to Great* and most everything from Simon Sinek and Malcolm Gladwell.

Becoming a successful advisor *did* build individual leadership skills, like how to build a plan and how to lead a family through financial decisions. But these were not the skills I needed to build and lead an infinite team.

There's a framework from Jim Collins and John Maxwell called The Five Levels of Leadership that maps out this journey.

### LEVEL ONE: THE HIGHLY CAPABLE INDIVIDUAL

Someone in a successful lifestyle practice is a highly capable individual. You know how to serve clients. You've built a practice through your own determination and skill. That's level one leadership.

### LEVEL TWO: CONTRIBUTING TEAM MEMBER

On this level, you're willing to work as a team to create something greater than the sum of its parts. You recognize that collaboration can achieve what you can't do alone.

## LEVEL THREE: COMPETENT MANAGER

Level three is about getting everyone rowing in the same direction toward specific goals. You're managing people, aligning efforts, and making sure the work gets done well.

## LEVEL FOUR: EFFECTIVE LEADER

Level four leaders create a cause that inspires people to do great work. It's not just about managing tasks anymore but creating meaning. People want to be part of what you're building.

## LEVEL FIVE: EXECUTIVE

At level five, you're mentoring and creating other level four leaders, so there's sustainability. You're building leaders who can build leaders. The company lives on beyond you.

Most successful lifestyle practices are excellent at level one. Some reach level two or three when they hire staff. But building an infinite team requires level four and five leadership.

That framework shows the destination. But here's the reality of living it.

## THE 5 LEVELS OF LEADERSHIP

**LEVEL 5** — **Level 5 Executive**

Builds enduring greatness through a paradoxical blend of personal humility and professional will.

**LEVEL 4** — **Effective Leader**

Catalyzes commitment to and vigorous pursuit of a clear and compelling vision, stimulating higher performance standards.

**LEVEL 3** — **Competent Manager**

Organizes people and resources toward the effective and efficient pursuit of predetermined objectives.

**LEVEL 2** — **Contributing Team Member**

Contributes individual capabilities to the achievement of group objectives and works effectively with others in a group setting.

**LEVEL 1** — **Highly Capable Individual**

Makes productive contributions through talent, knowledge, skills, and good work habits.

## I'M STILL ON THIS JOURNEY

In all honesty, I'm still on the journey.

How do I say less and ask more great questions? How do I flush out the truth of what's really going on in our organization and face the brutal facts when something isn't working? How do we get the right people on the bus and make tough decisions when we realize someone's in the wrong seat . . . or on the wrong bus entirely?

I didn't expect how much joy there is in watching someone else succeed in an area you helped nurture. Or how hard it is to stay quiet when you see someone struggling with something you could fix in five minutes. The patience this requires? Nobody warned me about that.

Now that we're well into our journey of building the infinite team, I sit back with true fascination and joy, realizing that something has been created that's larger than any individual and will continue well beyond our lifetime. There's a sense of gratitude and humility in that.

But the leader's journey never ends.

There will always be people who lose the forest through the trees, and you're there to help them see the bigger picture. There will always be people going through tough times, and you'll help them move forward for the betterment of the entire team or invite them to get off the bus if it's not working.

And one of those people someday might be yourself. In fact, it surely will. That's the point. Our careers as leaders and advisors will come to an end, and our team will live on to serve families.

## WHAT THIS SHIFT LOOKS LIKE

Remember how we talked about detaching clients from their advisor to the team? That change starts with you, personally.

When the team succeeds, you give them credit. When things go wrong, you take responsibility because the team is a reflection of its leaders.

You'll watch your own ideas get infused into the language of the company. Other people will teach your ideas to new team members who've forgotten where those ideas even came from.

And that's okay.

You'll watch people be passionate and inspired to do great work. They'll give credit to the coworker sitting beside them before they'll credit you for lighting the spark.

And that's okay, too.

You're no longer operating to build your own ego or benefit your own pocket. You're in service to give opportunities to other people to become great team members and great advisors who serve more families.

Our industry is wrapped up in individual achievement. People get addicted to seeing their names climb the charts. Their paychecks grow. More clients call them "my financial advisor."

Now I care about being built to last rather than ranking on charts. Rather than the highest assets per client, we have the highest percent of next-gen clients (the adult children). I used to have a dream of being retired and sipping a Mai Tai on some fancy beach somewhere. Now I dream of being retired and bumping into adult children of my clients who share how much their parents appreciated our support and how much they now rely on our team to make great financial decisions.

I hope that someday my name will be taken off the charts and replaced by our team name, giving credit where credit is due.

I hope I see that change during my career.

## MY OWN DOUBTS

When I faced the decision to transition from advisor to leader, I had my own doubts.

Could I be the leader I wanted to be? Could I lead a team to greatness? Would I enjoy building the next generation of advisors? Did I have the time and energy to develop the next chapter of our team?

When building a team, things get more complicated before they get easier. You have more people on the bus that you're trying to help see a future that doesn't exist yet. You're figuring out how everyone works together to get there.

When we started in this industry in 2000, our broker-dealer hired fifty people in our area. Only two of us survived. We heard thousands of nos as we asked thousands of people if they wanted to work with a financial advisor. We believed that someday, somehow, we would succeed.

That was challenging. It was hard. But it was all within our own determination to achieve it.

You might have heard of the three buckets of control.

**Bucket 1: Things you have complete control over.**

**Bucket 2: Things you can influence.**

**Bucket 3: Things you have no control over.**

A lifestyle business lives mostly in bucket one. An infinite team lives in bucket two.

That shift takes some getting used to.

You go from, "If I work hard enough, this will succeed," to, "If I lead well enough, we might succeed." That "might" is uncomfortable for people who built their practice through sheer determination and grit.

All you can do is guide the collaborative team and create an environment that fosters learning and growth. The rest? You have to let go.

I'm grateful to have started this next chapter in my mid-forties. I could not have imagined waiting any longer.

This is the biggest challenge of my career because the outcome is not within my control. I must lead, and believe, and let go.

## SO, WHERE DOES THIS LEAVE YOU?

If you've read this chapter and you're nodding along, recognizing that you genuinely enjoy developing people, that you're willing to shift from I to we, that you want to build something beyond your own career, you might be ready to build a team.

If you've read this chapter and you're thinking, *"This sounds exhausting, and I just want to focus on serving my best clients well."* Joining a team might be your path.

There is another powerful reason to join a team to serve as a value accelerator. Imagine a rockstar advisor who transitions the bottom half of their practice to a team's junior advisor bench. Imagine they focus their time and talent on more complex clients. Imagine that they also have leadership skills, and they help teach other junior advisors to be rockstars. Imagine if they have the talent to hold one of the C-suite roles (leadership responsibilities such as CEO, CFO, COO). I talked to one advisor who joined an elite team and sold 50 percent of his practice and continued to help the new team grow based on where they added the most value. They were enjoying the career more than ever. They have balance in life, and five years later, their remaining equity interest was worth more than their original business. Their value was accelerated, and so was the growth of the new team.

All options are valid choices.

There's no judgment here. The key is being honest with yourself about which path fits who you are and what you want from this next chapter of your career.

This is a big decision. It will shape the next decade or more of your life. It will affect your family, your team, and your clients. Take the time to really think through these questions.

Because once you've made that decision, you can move forward with clarity.

For those who decide to build, the next question becomes, "Where do you start? How do you create the foundation that everything else will be built upon?"

And that's where we're headed next.

CHAPTER 5

# BUILDING FROM THE INSIDE OUT: CREATING YOUR TEAM'S FOUNDATION

ABOUT SIX MONTHS AFTER we finalized our values and guiding principles, it happened.

Two team members came to me with completely opposing views on how to handle a client situation. Both were certain they were right. Both referenced our values to support their position.

One said, "Our value is service. We need to do whatever it takes for this client."

The other said, "Our value is sustainability. If we keep making exceptions, we're going to burn out the team."

They were both right. And they were waiting for me to decide.

That's when I realized that having values on the wall wasn't enough.

We could all agree that integrity, service, and teamwork mattered. But when we had to make actual decisions with competing priorities, we didn't know how to work through it together.

We needed more than shared beliefs. We needed to learn how to function as a team. In this chapter, we will walk through the essential first steps to establishing a team and how to grow together.

## WHEN YOU REALIZE YOU NEED HELP

I thought having values would solve our conflicts. Instead, it exposed them.

Before we had values, disagreements felt personal. After we had values, disagreements felt principled, but they were still disagreements. Maybe even more intense ones because now everyone felt justified.

We'd say things like, "I'm just trying to live our values," but we'd interpret those values differently based on our own wiring and experience.

So we brought in help.

We hired a consultant to take us through Patrick Lencioni's work on The Five Behaviors of a Cohesive Team. The Five Behaviors work taught us that having values isn't the same as knowing how to function as a team.

That requires different work.

Trust came first. Most people assume their team already

has trust. We did, too. But we had to learn the difference between trusting that someone will do their job and trusting them enough to admit mistakes, share weaknesses, and ask for help.

That required creating a safe, nonjudgmental space where vulnerability was okay.

Once we had trust, we could lean into healthy conflict. Many of us were conflict-avoidant. We'd rather let something slide than have a difficult conversation. We learned to give feedback directly, respectfully, and without making it personal.

I'll be honest. I'm still working on this one. When someone challenges one of my ideas, sometimes my first instinct is to explain why they're wrong and why I'm right. I have to consciously pause and ask, "What am I missing?"

Then came commitment, accountability, and results. Commitment meant supporting decisions even when they weren't your preference. Can you implement a system you didn't design? Can you support a decision you voted against? If the answer is no, you don't have commitment. You have compliance at best.

Accountability required learning to hold peers accountable for their commitments. We learned to reference our values when doing this. Instead of, "You're not pulling your weight," it becomes, "One of our values is teamwork, and when you miss deadlines, it affects the whole team. How can we help you meet your commitments?"

It's still uncomfortable. But it's a lot more productive.

Results tied it all together. When trust, conflict, commitment, and accountability are in place, teams can focus on collective results. Not my results. Not your results. Our results. But this required letting go of some things I'd been holding onto.

## WHEN IT FINALLY CLICKS

About a year into this process, I overheard two team members talking. One was sharing a story about a client meeting that had gone particularly well. She was animated, excited.

"It just felt good, you know? I felt empowered to make that call without having to check with anyone first. And I think we really created a story there, something that the family will remember."

The other team member nodded. "That's exactly what we're trying to do. Every interaction creates a story."

Have you ever had an experience that fulfilled a dream or goal you didn't know you had? That was one of those moments for me.

She'd just quoted one of our guiding principles without even realizing it. More importantly, she was living it, using it to make sense of her work, to celebrate what had gone well, to reinforce what mattered.

This wasn't a team meeting where I was cheerleading values. This wasn't a performance review where someone was trying to say the right thing. This was just two people talking in the break room, and our culture had become the lens through which they saw their work.

## MAKING STRUCTURE DECISIONS

Now that we knew how to work together, we had to decide what we were building. What kind of team, with what structure, and why.

So what does an infinite team look like? We had to figure out four main roles.

### SHAREHOLDERS

Elite teams need equity shareholders with an invested interest in making sure the entity grows and survives. Not just employees collecting a paycheck, but people who have skin in the game for the long term.

The questions we faced were "Who gets to be a shareholder? How do you earn it? What's the pathway?"

It's not just about tenure or revenue but who's truly invested in the infinite journey, who's thinking beyond their own career, who's building for what comes after them. In our industry, only licensed advisors can have equity in a business due to SEC rules.

### C-SUITE LEADERS

One person can't do it all. The solo practitioner tries to be CEO, CFO, COO, and everything else. One financial advisor can try to wear all the hats, but this ultimately creates a ceiling of what a team can or cannot become.

As we built the team, we had to let people specialize in their domains. I had to trust that someone else could run operations better than I could. Someone else could train on systems better than I could.

That was harder than I expected.

## THE ADVISOR FORCE

Then you need advisors, the people who serve families. You need lead advisors who are seasoned veterans, and junior advisors learning the craft and building their careers.

Some teams form what are called Diamond Teams, which are smaller teams within the larger team that are structured around a lead advisor. One elite advisor might have one or two junior advisors working with them, plus an operations team member.

## THE SUPPORT TEAM

Then you need the employees who keep the wheels turning: operations, client service, marketing, technology support, and more.

These roles are not secondary. They're not "just support." They're essential team members who enable the advisors to do what they do best.

When we started treating "support roles" with the same importance as advisor roles, when we included them in the values process, in the Five Behaviors work, in the compensation discussions, they went from feeling like they worked for the advisors to feeling like they were part of the team.

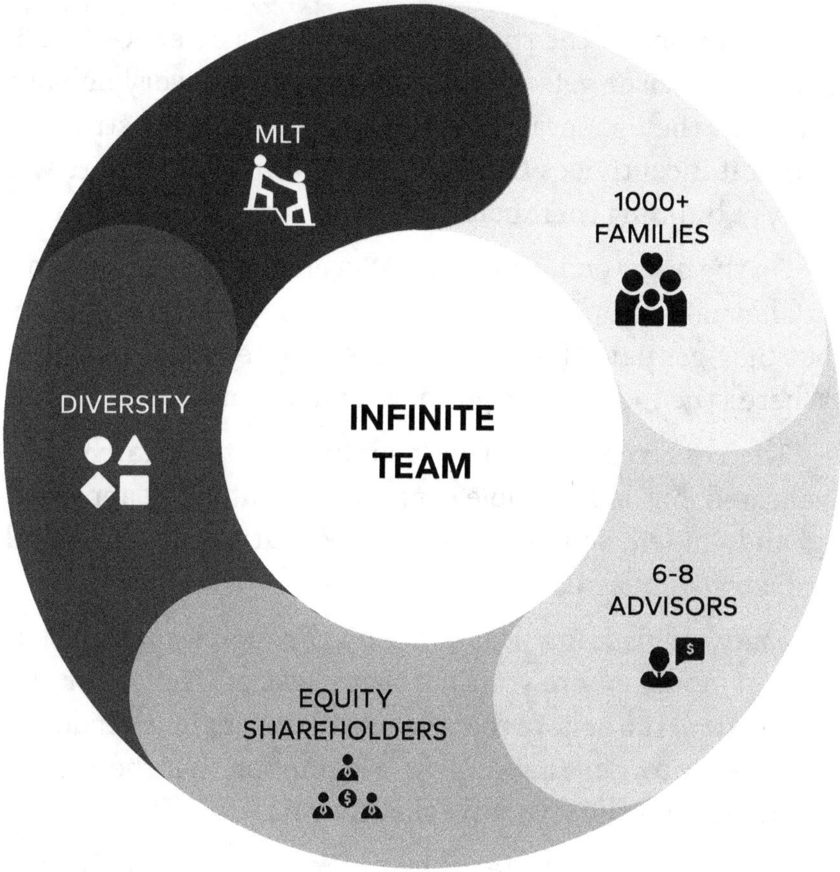


## ALIGNING COMPENSATION WITH VALUES

When I built my practice, I used an "eat what you kill" model. So my first instinct was to assume that's what would motivate everyone else.

I was wrong.

## THE COMPENSATION CONTINUUM

I've researched dozens of teams. There's variability in compensation structures with no clear right answer.

On one end of the spectrum, you have a direct GDC split. A junior advisor gets an exact percentage of every dollar of business they generate. The challenge with this structure is that it incentivizes the junior advisor to put "I before we." They're building their book, not the team.

On the other end, you have a W-2 employee with no bonus or alternate compensation program. They're all about team, but they get paid the same whether the team grows or not. Where's the incentive to go above and beyond?

The research shows that people want to be fairly compensated, but most people care more about being appreciated and valued, so long as the compensation is in line with industry standards.

Many advisor-owners came up through a commission-driven model where your paycheck was entirely your own production. I do believe there's a misalignment in the industry, with many owners making the assumption that their junior advisors want the structure that they had.

This creates a splintered team that will ultimately grow slower than a unified elite team.

So we had to find somewhere in the middle.

## WHAT WORKS FOR US

We target the seventy-fifth percentile or higher, according to compensation studies in our region, for everyone who's been with us three-plus years and doing great work. That's our baseline.

Then everyone gets a bonus rated zero, one, two, or three, a percentage of salary tied to contribution, not whether we had a good year. Zero means you did your job well, and there's nothing wrong with that. One, two, or three means you went beyond.

Junior advisors can earn additional bonuses tied to specific goals we agree on together, such as new clients, insurance business, and other milestones.

If everyone is fairly compensated with a bonus program aligned with team growth, and we all work together, then one plus one plus one *can* equal four.

A faster-growing team creates more opportunities for everyone. Not just the partners. Everyone.

We're still refining this. We test it. We get feedback. We adjust.

But the principle holds. Compensation must align with values, or the values are just words on a wall.

## WHAT GOT YOU HERE WILL NOT GET YOU THERE

Think about the characteristics that make someone running a lifestyle practice great. They're very driven, competitive, smart, and detailed. They control all their variables. They work harder than anyone else.

But your biggest strength can be a weakness.

When someone running a lifestyle practice becomes wildly successful, they're almost forced to create a team. But their strongest qualities become barriers to building a great team.

Here's what I had to unlearn:

- I had to stop believing I was the smartest person in the room (because I wasn't). A true leader focuses on growing a great team, hires smarter people, and allows them to make decisions. I had to let go of control. That meant tolerating mistakes I wouldn't have made. Watching someone struggle with something I could fix quickly but knowing they need to figure it out themselves;
- I had to shift from working harder to working smarter. That meant getting everyone rowing in the same direction instead of just rowing harder, myself. This meant slowing down to ensure everyone was on board before I leaped ahead.

Successful advisors tend to let go of control too late. They hold too much. They hide their shortcomings. They hire people less talented than themselves and then are disappointed but feel good that they continue to be the smartest person on the team.

For the first half of our careers, we got used to being praised and awarded for individual success. As you build a team, you award the successes of others.

You want to inspire and motivate team members to do great work. In the process of creating a compensation and reward structure that supports that, you let go of your own need to be rewarded.

Your reward becomes intrinsic. You're simply satisfied knowing that others are achieving great results for their careers and their families, regardless of whether you are acknowledged for your part in the journey.

My wife uses a phrase that I love: *"Catch people in the act of awesome."*

It is rewarding when your team knows you're looking for their wins and they trust that you're celebrating their successes instead of waiting for their mistakes.

You are playing a different "game." As Simon Sinek said, "You are playing an infinite game."

## THE FOUNDATION IS MORE THAN VALUES

The foundation of an infinite team is more than just values. Values tell you what you stand for; learning to work as a team teaches you how to stand together.

The values, the teamwork, the structure, and the compensation aligned with purpose are all just preparation.

The real test comes when you start bringing new advisors onto the team. How do you find them? How do you train them? How do you ensure they carry this culture forward?

Because you can build the most beautiful foundation in the world, but if you can't develop the next generation of advisors who will stand on it, you're still just building a lifestyle practice with more people.

And that's where we're headed next.

CHAPTER 6

# THE ADVISOR BENCH: DEVELOPING YOUR NEXT GENERATION

WE HIRED FOUR JUNIOR advisors before we stopped to evaluate what wasn't working.

Two came from absorbing advisors from a prior office. They were never really embedded with our team. That didn't work out.

One came from an insurance background. They didn't have the mindset of a fee-based financial advisor and wealth manager. That didn't work out either.

One came in with no background but wanted to be a partner immediately. That didn't work out.

We failed enough times that we seriously thought about giving up on building an advisor bench.

I thought building an infinite team meant getting clear on values and creating systems. Those things mattered. But the hardest part isn't the strategy. It's finding people who can do the work and then developing them into advisors who serve families the way you do by meeting our standard of care.

You can have the best values in the world. You can create beautiful systems. But you need to develop the people who will carry it forward.

In this chapter, we'll explore what matters when hiring advisors, how we structure training that builds real competence, the balance between guidance and freedom, and why moving slower helps you grow faster.

## WHAT I WISH I'D KNOWN ABOUT HIRING

When I hired my first junior advisor, I looked for someone smart, driven, good with people, and analytical. Pretty standard stuff.

Then I hired two more advisors who were almost identical. They had the same energy, the same interests, and the same strengths.

Then I realized I was hiring people like me.

But I didn't need more of the same; I needed diversity. Not just diversity in gender and backgrounds, though that matters. I'm talking about diversity in what energizes different advisors. What they get excited about. What type of clients they want to serve.

Some advisors love working with young families just getting started. They see themselves in those clients. They enjoy helping someone make their first real financial decisions.

Other advisors prefer working with retirees. They have the patience for Medicare questions and thrive in legacy conversations.

Some advisors want to build a large practice and have a pathway to partnership someday. Others are content serving families well and appreciate the stability of a steady paycheck.

Many talented people want to be advisors but have zero interest in being business owners.

They don't want to solve complex team problems. They don't want the responsibility of overseeing people. They don't want to chart into unknown waters and get people excited to follow them through a storm. They don't want to wear one hundred hats.

They just want to do great work for families.

Those people can be exceptional team members. But you'll never attract them if you only talk about entrepreneurship.

| TARGET MARKET | | | | | |
|---|---|---|---|---|---|
| Market Group | Newer/Older Investor | | Core Target Market | | Higher Net Worth |
| | Seekers/Achievers/ Children | Legacy / Retired clients | Seekers / HNW Accumulators | Legacy / More complex retirees | Complex |
| Total Asset Level | Under $1MM | Under $1MM | $1-10MM | $1-10MM | $10MM+ |
| Advisor Type | AFA | | Senior Advisor | | Sr. Advisor w/ CFA support |
| CSM Level | Bronze/Silver | Silver & G2 | Platinum & G1 | G1 & Platinum | Platinum+ |
| Needs | Financial education, establish systematic savings, life & disability insurance, build CR, debt management, CF analysis, 401k review, employee benefit review, basic estate planning concepts | Asset management, risk management, distribution plan, tax strategy, soc. Sec. analysis, RMD planning, QCD planning, LTC planning, multi gen discuss, estate planning | Deep level of financial edu., build wealth tax efficiently, IPS with risk tol. & inv. Pref., tax planning, estate planning, retirement planning, stock option/ equity analysis, what if scenarios, protection planning | Investment Reviews, Risk Management, income distribution plan, 30-year income map, tax strategy/ RMD/QCD/lifestyle needs, Legacy planning, multi-gen, estate planning (AMP POA) | Same needs as Target Market. More attention, more coordination with professionals. Additional needs could include philanthropy. |
| Advisor Skills | CFP – financial planning and insurance specialist | Experience with older clients, investment review, distribution strategies (inv/tax), basic estate planning knowledge, next gen discussion and introduction | Complex financial planning, tax efficient wealth building strategies, tax and legal knowledge, CPA/ Attorney coordination, stock options/equity transition | Complex ret. planning, giving strategies, roth conver., income distribution, SSA, QCD, RMD, LTC, Estate Planning, Multi-Gen disc., Next-gen introduction | Same skills as senior advisor. White glove service. Fully vetted and tailored. Full team experience w/ full support of CFA/AFA. |

## TRAINING PROGRAMS: THEN VS. NOW

Twenty years ago, large corporations did the heavy lifting. They trained young advisors, and then those advisors would eventually move out into the field and join teams like ours.

Then the Fortune 500 companies decided they weren't going to invest in training programs the same way anymore. Teams had to figure it out themselves.

So now you have two options. Home-grow your people from intern to team member to paraplanner to associate advisor to lead advisor. Or recruit seasoned advisors.

Neither path is easy.

Home growing takes tremendous infrastructure. You need the right systems, training programs, and mentorship capacity. And even then, most won't make it.

If you recruit experienced advisors, you're bringing in someone with well-formed ideas about how things should work. Can you teach an old dog new tricks? Will they adopt your methods, or will they keep doing what they've always done?

We decided our likelihood of success would increase if we invested in growing our own.

Really, it was the only way to build the culture we wanted.

## BUILDING FROM SCRATCH

So, we launched an internship program. But more importantly, we gained clarity on how teams build talent.

As you can see, the most upstream activity comes from building relationships with institutions that funnel their top talent to your internship program, which leads to successful interns. Great interns can become great team members. Great team members can become great advisors.

**INFINITE TEAM MODEL**

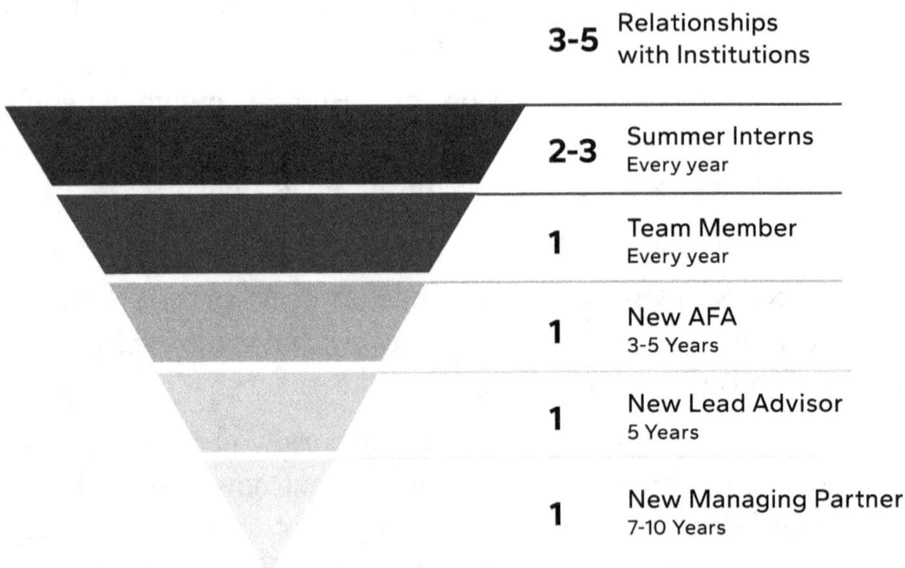


So what did we build? Here's the structure we put in place to support that pipeline:

**The 500-Foot View Map** - Maps out the space and time we need to teach and train advisors. It's a visual representation, so everyone can see the journey from intern to lead advisor.

**The Advisor Grid** - Outlines the skills advisors need at different stages. Junior advisors can see exactly what they're building toward. Lead advisors can assess where someone needs development.

## Advisor Career Progression

| Category | Intern | Paraplanner | Paraplanner (Chair 2) | AFA (Servicing 1) | AFA (Servicing 2) | AFA (Servicing 3) | AFA (Lead Advisor) | Managing Partner |
|---|---|---|---|---|---|---|---|---|
| Public Title<br>Internal Title | Intern<br>Intern | Paraplanner<br>Concierge | Paraplanner (Chair 2)<br>Chair 2 (% Concierge/ % Chair 2) | AFA (Servicing 1)<br>Servicing AFA 1 | AFA (Servicing 2)<br>Servicing AFA 2 | AFA (Servicing 3)<br>Servicing AFA 3 | AFA (Lead Advisor)<br>Lead Advisor | Managing Partner<br>Lead Advisor/ Owner |
| Key Responsibilities | FP/Meeting Prep Support, Business Projects, Learning & Development, Capstone | Complete meeting planner follow-up tasks; Execute trades and money movement requests; Assist clients with form completion, account transfers, questions/concerns, etc. | Continue to execute paraplanner duties; Provide Chair 2 support; Learn advisor tools: emeeting, CSM, MGP, insurance, etc.; Attend Advisor trainings; Advisor project support; Protection Support | Assigned a small book of clients: 50-75 clients; 150-300k GDC; Partial access to concierge team; Execute practice CSM; Growth track to AFA Level 2: 1-2M net flows, 15+ prospects, 10+ new clients; Own a specialty: Insurance, Compliance, Licensing | All expectations of level 1 plus: 350-500k GDC; 100-200 clients; Partial access to concierge team; Growth track to level 3 Advisor: 2M+ net flows, 20+ referrals, 10+ new clients (50% HVC); COI development, 20 referrals per year or track outreach | All expectations of level 2 plus: 500-750k GDC; 150-200 clients; Full access to concierge team; Growth track to Senior Advisor: 3M+ net flows, 20+ referrals, 10+ new clients (50% HVC); Team expert in specific area | All expectations of level 3 plus: 750k+ GDC; 150-250 clients; Strong COI relationships; Lead/ Teach AFAs within area of expertise (planning, investments, insurance, marketing, new business); 5M net flows, 20+ referrals, 10+ new clients (50% HVC); 12 COI meetings/ year | All expectations of lead advisor plus: 1M+ GDC; 50-200 clients; C-suite duties; 24 COI Meetings per year |
| Teaching Hospital Responsibilities | Emma & Teddy are responsible for recruitment and training | Jeff is responsible for training and implementation of concierge group | Level 1&2 AFAs train chair 2 on all systems/tools such as: MGP, MP, FRS, etc. | AFA level 2&3 train on CSM and onboarding 101; Partners train and observe for proficiency | Platinum joint case work; Partners train and observe for proficiency | Platinum joint case work; Partners train and observe for proficiency | | Partners/C-Suite receives coaching/consulting from XFA and Jambalaya |

**Structured Learning** - We pay for education and CFP designations, advisor training twice per month, and opportunities to enroll in broker-dealer training and conferences. We encourage team members to form best-practice groups with their peers on other teams. We also hire two consulting firms to provide coaching to our team as part of their training and development. We provide access to conferences that are available when applicable.

**The Teaching Hospital Model** - Here's how it works:

Each layer of the organization has the opportunity to learn and grow to the next level. They also have the responsibility to teach and train the group rising up behind them.

Our intern from the past two summers is starting full-time this summer. She'll oversee and run the internship program.

Our junior advisors help train younger concierge and operations team members who want to become advisors someday. They teach the "science" of the advisor business.

Lead advisors with more than ten years of experience teach our level 1 and 2 junior advisors the "art" side of the business. They sit in on meetings and observe junior advisors.

Partners guide lead advisors to become better leaders and prepare for an ownership stake in the company.

Junior advisors serve as "chair two" for new client onboarding. They observe. Then we observe them. Then they practice on their own.

## MATCHING PEOPLE TO FAMILIES

Once you have invested in and trained up junior advisors, you need a plan for matching them with the right clients.

We look at three things: client needs, advisor experience and passion, and personality fit. We've identified five primary target markets our advisors serve:

1. Young families building wealth
2. High-net-worth achievers
3. Retirees with modest assets
4. High-net-worth retirees
5. Complex business owners

We match advisors to the clients they naturally connect with and the life stage they understand best.

A twenty-eight-year-old advisor with young kids might work primarily with other young families. They speak the same language, and they understand the challenges.

The retirement transition may be the most important financial decision clients make during their lifetime. A lead advisor is better prepared to help families through this transition as they have helped more than one hundred families through the same process. A less experienced advisor can pull a lead advisor into the meetings for additional support as they help their clients transition.

Small business owners are an entirely different group. Ideally, an advisor has the CEPA designation and other related experience.

This doesn't mean advisors only work with one group. But having a primary focus allows them to develop real expertise instead of being a generalist trying to serve everyone.

## FINDING THE SWEET SPOT

One of the most challenging aspects of building an elite team is the sweet spot between a structured process to follow and the freedom to discover for themselves, or what we call "Freedom in a Box." People don't want to be controlled; they want to feel they have some freedom and flexibility.

We're still working on this.

If you micromanage, you stifle growth. If you delegate too quickly, you lose institutional knowledge.

There's a saying, *"Delegation without inspection is abdication."*

We have a master spreadsheet that outlines all the skills an advisor needs. We have a process where junior advisors observe lead advisors, lead advisors observe junior advisors, and then junior advisors try it themselves and report back.

But it is human nature to delegate too quickly. We don't want to spend the time shadowing and observing over and over. We want to hand something off and move on, which can be a mistake.

The Navy SEALs have a saying, "Slow is smooth. Smooth is fast." This emphasizes the importance of precision and control in high-pressure situations. By focusing on deliberate, smooth movements, you achieve greater speed and accuracy when it matters most.

When we move slowly with junior advisors, investing the time to guide them properly, they can develop skills in five to ten years that took us ten to twenty years to figure out on our own. By joining a team, you can get there faster than you can on your own.

If we transfer clients and delegate too quickly, they'll trip and stumble just like we did. And it will take them just as long.

## WHAT KEEPS PEOPLE

So you've found great advisors. You've trained them. You've invested years developing their skills.

How do you make sure they stay?

Most advisors think retention is about compensation. Make the numbers work, and people stay. Get the bonus structure right. Offer a pathway to partnership. Check the boxes.

I thought that, too.

Then I went to a conference, and a consultant walked through how much time leaders should spend on leadership based on the size of their team. He had it all mapped out. If you have this many advisors, you should be spending this percentage of your time leading them, not just serving clients.

Everyone in the room was shocked.

The consultant was basically saying, if you want to build and keep a great team, leadership isn't something you do a halfday a week between client meetings. It's the majority of your job.

I was the leader of the smallest team in that room. And I was spending 50 percent of my time on leadership in building culture, developing people, and making sure everyone's rowing in the same direction.

Everyone thought I was crazy.

But what I've learned is that poor retention doesn't usually happen because someone got a better offer somewhere else. It happens because of poor communication and bad leadership.

If we're open and transparent with our people, if we take time to really learn and listen to them, most issues can be resolved. Most individualized career plans can align with both the firm's goals and the person's goals.

But that requires time.

It requires building a culture where people feel known. Where they see a path forward for themselves. Where the values you spent a year defining show up in how you treat each other every single day.

You can't build something that lasts if you're not willing to invest the time in the people who will carry it forward.

## WHAT THIS LOOKS LIKE WHEN IT WORKS

Now, all of this might sound theoretical. Let me show you what it looks like when it works.

Sarah[2] came to us from a recruiting firm. She'd already had an internship on a different team. We hired her as an operations specialist. For three years, she worked to learn our team, our systems, our values, our people, our clients, and the team way.

We began having Sarah sit in meetings and shadow lead advisors. She worked extremely hard to get all the licenses needed, including the CFP, in preparation for becoming an advisor.

When the opportunity presented itself, we flipped the switch.

We assigned Sarah thirty clients and began onboarding new families together with lead advisors. For another year, she played a "chair two" role, participating in client meetings, working through presentations, and helping families implement solutions.

Then we began giving her opportunities to present and dialogue with clients herself while we observed and provided feedback.

Sarah's now in her second year as an advisor. She's developed a specialty in insurance, which was a need on our team. She helps onboard new families with support from lead advisors. Many of these families are children of clients we already serve.

She's learning new skills at a fast pace, helping real families, implementing real insurance cases and rollover opportunities.

Sarah's story makes it sound straightforward. But even with the internship program, the structured training, the mentorship, and the systems, most people won't make it.

Back in the 1990s and 2000s, big broker-dealers recruited hundreds of people. Less than 2 percent survived.

The odds haven't changed that much.

You can do everything right and still lose talented people. Some will realize this career isn't for them. Some will get better opportunities elsewhere. Some will move for family reasons.

That's why you need a bench. That's why the internship program matters. You're constantly sifting through, identifying the cream of the crop, and grooming the ones who show real promise.

It's not efficient. It's not quick.

But it's the only way to build something that lasts.

## SO WHAT DOES THIS MEAN FOR YOU?

If you're considering building a team with an advisor bench, ask yourself:

- Am I willing to invest years before seeing results?
- Do I have the patience to shadow the same person over and over while they learn?
- Can I tolerate junior advisors making mistakes I wouldn't make?
- Am I prepared to build training systems, track development, and provide constant feedback?
- Do I genuinely enjoy watching others succeed, even when they're not as good as I am yet?

If you answered no to most of those questions, that's okay. Joining a team might be your better path. But if you answered yes, if you're energized by the idea of developing the next generation, then understand this is a long-term play. Fortunately, we began this journey in our mid-forties. I personally don't believe someone in their sixties has the runway to build an infinite team.

The advisors you're training today won't be ready to take over significant client relationships for five to ten years. Maybe longer.

But when they are ready? When you've built a bench of talented advisors who understand your values, who've learned your methods, who care about serving families the way you do?

That's when the infinite team becomes real.

That's when you can start thinking about transitions without panic. When you can specialize instead of being a generalist. When you can serve three generations of one family because you have advisors who specialize in each stage of life.

But none of that happens if you can't develop the people who will make it possible.

In the next chapter, we will talk about what happens when you hand a client relationship you spent fifteen years building to someone who's been an advisor for two years and how you can protect those relationships during the transition.

CHAPTER 7

# CLIENT-CENTRIC TRANSITIONS: PROTECTING RELATIONSHIPS THROUGH CHANGE

I HAD A PROBLEM.

I'd spent fifteen years building relationships with these families. They trusted me with everything. Their retirement savings, their kids' college funds, and the wealth they'd worked their entire lives to build.

Now I was supposed to hand them over to advisors who'd been in the business for five years. How was that supposed to work?

Every successful person running a lifestyle practice faces this moment eventually. You've built something valuable, and your clients love working with you, and that's exactly what makes this so hard.

The same relationships that made your practice successful are now the barrier to building something that lasts.

In this chapter, I'm going to walk you through how we did this. The process we figured out, the language that worked, the concerns clients raised, and how we addressed them. And how we know it's working.

## IT WAS HARDER THAN I THOUGHT

I need to be honest up front. This was hard. Harder than I expected. I had to allow myself to consider that another advisor could be trained to serve these families as well as I did or perhaps even better.

I had to consider that there were plenty of other advisors with similar experience and skill. That my clients didn't need me, specifically. They needed great advice and great service, which other people could also provide.

For fifteen years, I'd believed I was the best person to serve my clients. That belief drove me to build a great practice. But that same belief became the barrier in my transition from I to we.

So once I got over my own ego, which took longer than I'd like to admit, we could finally build what was needed. Not a plan to replace me but a process to transition relationships without breaking trust.

## MAKING THE SHIFT

To make this shift, we developed a process. It took three years of trial and error, but it was worth it because this process works!

## BEFORE WE COULD TRANSITION ANYONE, WE HAD TO DO SOME FOUNDATIONAL WORK.

We worked to deepen clients' relationships with the entire team, not just with me. We wanted to see a shift in their language from, "Ben's my guy" to, "This team is the firm that helps my family."

That didn't happen overnight. Over two to three years, we spent fifteen to twenty minutes in each client meeting, sharing our team's story. Who we were becoming. Why we were building a team. What it meant for their family.

Meanwhile, we were building the associate advisor bench by training people who could handle these transitions when the time came.

So by the time we had the transition conversation, clients already understood what we were building. They'd heard the story. They'd met the team. They'd seen us evolving from a practice built around me to a firm built around a purpose.

That foundation made everything else possible.

## NEXT, CLIENTS HAVE TO SEE THE ASSOCIATE ADVISOR AS PART OF THEIR TEAM.

The associate advisor joins client meetings. They don't sit silently in the corner, but they participate in the conversation, and they help implement solutions. They're an active part of serving the family.

Within a meeting or two, the client develops a relationship with the associate advisor.

## THEN, CREATE OPPORTUNITIES FOR THE ASSOCIATE ADVISOR TO REACH OUT INDEPENDENTLY.

We'd have the associate advisor make quarterly or semi-annual check-in calls. If something came up mid-year that needed action, the associate advisor would reach out.

These small touches build trust over time, so that by the time we positioned the change, the client already had a decent relationship with the new advisor. They weren't meeting them for the first time in the transition conversation. We are looking for an opportunity for the junior advisor to provide advice to the client

## FIND THE APPROPRIATE TIMING FOR THE TRANSITION.

You don't want to make changes when clients are going through major life transitions. It is a bad idea to do this with a family dealing with a health crisis, or if someone is retiring in six months. You want to wait for a time when they're settled.

We learned this by screwing it up. We tried to transition a client right as they were dealing with a parent's declining health. They were stressed, emotional, and not in a place to hear about changes. It didn't go well.

So now we pay attention. What's happening in their life? What transitions are they navigating? Sometimes the right answer is to wait.

## POSITION THE ASSOCIATE ADVISOR AS THE NEW POINT OF CONTACT.

Notice that language: point of contact.

Not "new advisor." Not "taking over your account." Point of contact.

We learned this through trial and error. We'd say "we're changing your advisor" and watch clients' faces fall. They heard, "You're getting downgraded."

So we changed the language. "We would like [Junior Advisor's name] to be your primary point of contact," landed completely differently. Same change, but clients didn't feel like they were losing something.

In practice, the conversation often sounds something like this:

"As we've grown the team, I'm taking on more of a leadership role and working with fewer families directly. Would you be open to having [advisor name] be your primary point of contact? I'll still be available as needed, but they will be taking the lead on your service meetings and be your primary resource when you have questions or concerns throughout the year."

Then we'd explain why. Not just, "I'm busy." But the real reason. "This allows me to focus on leading the team, so we can continue serving your family for decades to come. It ensures we have the capacity to help your children when they're ready."

Most clients understand this reasoning.

### CHECK IN OVER THE NEXT YEAR.

We don't just make the switch and disappear.

We have a team member make random follow-up calls to check on the client's experience. This call is made by a neutral team member who can hear honest feedback.

We also review client satisfaction surveys and track those responses closely. Are they getting the service they need? Is the relationship working? What could we improve?

If we see patterns like clients leaving or satisfaction dropping, we know something's wrong and can course correct.

### BRING THE LEAD ADVISOR BACK IN WHEN NEEDED.

When something complicated comes up, like a big inheritance, a business sale, or a complex estate planning issue, the associate advisor will pull the lead advisor back into the meeting.

When we do this, we assure the client that we're still working as a team. It solidifies the new relationship and the team cohesiveness.

The client sees, "Oh, they really meant it when they said they're still available. This isn't abandonment. It's a team approach."

Bringing the lead advisor back in for something complex proves you meant what you said.

## WHAT CLIENTS ARE WORRIED ABOUT

Even when clients understand the rationale, they'd rather keep working with you. Their concerns tend to cluster around a few themes.

They're concerned their service will change, that they'll get less attention, slower responses, or that their meetings will get canceled or rescheduled. They're concerned their investments will change, that the new advisor will mess with what's working. They're concerned they won't have somebody as responsive, that emails will go unanswered or questions will take longer to get addressed. They're concerned they won't like the new advisor. Chemistry matters, and they're worried about starting over with someone new. They're concerned the new advisor doesn't know as much as you, questioning competence, even if they won't say it out loud.

The concern underneath it all is, "Do you still care about me?"

That's the question your explanation needs to answer. When you frame the transition around building something that will serve their family for life, most clients hear the right thing. And I always tell them to bring any feedback directly to me if the transition has impacted their service in any way.

## WHEN IT WORKS

Richard and Marian[3] were in their early seventies. They were retired educators who had saved well and had substantial assets. We had navigated a complicated transition to retirement together; their portfolios were stable, and they were in what I call maintenance mode.

But they kept asking me to help their adult children who lived out of state.

I explained that my office had evolved into a much larger team and that I was taking on more of a leadership role and working with fewer families directly.

Then I asked them, "Now that you're through the challenging retirement transition, would you be open to working with one of our other advisors as your primary point of contact? This would free me up to focus on building the team, and it would give us capacity to help your children."

They were uncomfortable at first. But we'd spent a year building their relationship with the new advisor. They'd been in meetings together, and they'd experienced the associate advisor's competence and responsiveness.

So they agreed to try it.

After about six months, they thanked me for finding a way to make sure the team could continue serving their family, and then they referred their children to us.

Today, they receive great service from an associate advisor who has more time for them. Their children are working with our firm, and we've become part of a multi-generational family.

Every Thanksgiving, we send Richard and Marian a centerpiece for their table. And somewhere between the meal and the conversation, our firm comes up. Wisdom passed along to children, grandchildren, and anyone else gathered around.

And when the children grow, have good jobs, get married, and have kids of their own, they reach out and say, "I'm so excited to finally meet you. I've heard about you for years!"

## WHAT I WISH I'D KNOWN

If I could go back and tell myself anything before we started this process, here's what I'd say:

Start building the foundation earlier. We waited too long to shift clients' perception from me to the team. The earlier you start, the easier the transitions become.

Be more patient with timing. We rushed a few transitions because we were eager to scale. Those were the ones that struggled. The ones where we waited for the right moment? Those went smoothly.

Invest more time in the relationship-building phase. The months where the associate advisor joins meetings before the transition is not wasted time. It is one of the most important parts. Clients are more comfortable transitioning to someone they already know. To prove this point, I found that it was easier to transition a client to a level 2 AFA who they already knew than it was to transition them to my business partner of twenty-five years (who they didn't know).

Trust the process, even when it feels uncomfortable. And accept that some clients will never fully embrace the change. And that's okay.

Several years into this, I can tell you transitions still aren't easy. But they're easier than they were when we started. The process works when we follow it. We don't rush the timing anymore. We invest in the relationship-building phase. And when something doesn't feel right, we wait. But a very important distinction is that we are waiting when it is not a good time for the client. If it is you who isn't ready to let go, this is another thing entirely!

The hardest part isn't the process. It's accepting that your clients don't need you, specifically. They need great service, which a well-trained team can provide. That's a bitter pill to swallow. But it's also the pill that sets you free to build something bigger than yourself. Something that lasts beyond your career. Something that is greater than oneself. Something infinite.

## SO, WHERE DOES THIS LEAVE YOU?

The transition conversations get easier when you've spent years preparing clients to think about their relationship with you and your team differently.

But even with all this preparation, transitions remain one of the hardest parts of building an infinite team because you're asking clients to trust that something new can be as good as what they already love.

In the next chapter, we are going to cover how to build a multigenerational practice that serves families across decades. How the whole system comes together when you get this right.

Because client transitions aren't the end goal. They're the bridge to something bigger.

CHAPTER 8

# GENERATIONS OF FAMILIES: BUILDING A MULTIGENERATIONAL PRACTICE

JOE[4] CALLED ME ONE day after he had found out that he was the executor of his father's estate.

He was clearly stressed. His father, Albert, wanted to make his own decisions, but he was starting to become forgetful. Assets were scattered across multiple accounts. Neither of them could get their arms around what they had.

They were also worried about how they would pay for long-term care for Albert if he needed it. It seemed to Joe that the day might come sooner than he was ready for. How would they pay for it? What options did they have?

As we dug in, we discovered Albert had a long-term care policy he didn't even remember. We changed the agent to our office so we could help coordinate care when the time came.

We also noticed that Albert made a $100 monthly donation to his church. We recommended doing a Qualified Charitable Distribution from Albert's IRA instead, saving him money on taxes.

The meeting showed us that Joe trusted us with the care of his father.

That's multigenerational planning. Not a strategy session about generational wealth transfer. A son and his aging father, both stressed, are trying to figure out how to navigate what comes next. And a team that could help them.

You can't do this in a lifestyle practice. You need advisors who understand Medicare, long-term care, estate execution, and tax-efficient giving. You need time to dig through scattered accounts and find the policies no one remembered. You need the capacity to take on a relationship that might not generate significant revenue but matters deeply to a family you've served for years.

So let's talk about how the "Invested in Family" mantra translates into actual services, what systems make this work without burning out your team, and what success looks like when you get this right.

## WHAT DIFFERENT GENERATIONS NEED

With the team structure in place, including the values, the advisors, and the training systems, our mantra shapes how we make decisions.

Most firms ask, "Can we help them? Do they have enough money?"

We ask, "How can we help them? What do they need right now?"

A thirty-year-old starting their career needs different things than their parents navigating retirement. Not less. Different. They need education and basic planning. Their parents need sophisticated investment, tax, and estate planning work.

And then there's the other end of the spectrum. Our mantra also pushes us to help parents of clients in their eighties and nineties. Maybe they've lost a spouse who ran the personal finances, and they need support. Whether or not they move assets isn't the point. It's simply the right thing to do.

These parents might not meet typical minimums. They might not generate significant revenue. But when their fifty-five-year-old child sees us caring for their aging parent with the same attention we give to million-dollar clients, they know what kind of team we are. And that adult child (our actual client) will be incredibly grateful.

A mentor once told me, "In this business, you want the mind of a capitalist and the heart of a social worker."

Service to families is the ultimate inspiration. The monetary reward matters. But in the back half of a successful career, you realize it isn't the ultimate goal.

Still, we needed to protect our team's capacity and resources. We can't promise every client the same service model regardless of their situation. We had to get clear on what we could sustainably provide.

Parents with millions of dollars want their children to receive great service. They also understand their twenty-eight-year-old needs something different from what they do.

It's the art of positioning.

I remember the first time a parent asked about this. I explained, "Our team is committed to helping your daughter. We've designed a level of service that fits where she is in life. As her situation becomes more complex, the service can grow with her. This allows us to help your kids without impacting what we provide you."

They said yes.

They always say yes when you're honest about what you can and can't provide.

## HOW WE START THESE CONVERSATIONS

So, how do you engage with clients' adult children effectively? Our primary approach is a process we call *Share "Our Story."*

During client meetings, we ask a lot of questions. How were your holidays? Who did you enjoy spending time with? What fun experiences did you have? And then, later in the meeting, we ask value-seeking questions. Did you find this meeting valuable? What did you find most valuable? As we confirm the client is finding value in this experience, we let them know we're happy to be a resource for the family/friends that they spent time with over the holidays. Something like, "You mentioned earlier that your daughter, her husband, and new baby traveled to your home for the holidays. As they build their new family and move into their new home, please know that we are happy to be a resource for any financial questions they may have along the way."

We listen for what we call triggering events in family members' lives:

- Buying a first home;
- Having a baby;
- Changing jobs;
- Death or disability of a spouse;
- Growth or sale of a business;
- Planning for or transitioning to retirement;
- Aging parents beginning to need care.

We've also developed summer campaigns where interns send emails and follow up with phone calls. We have offered complimentary consultations and free financial education for clients' children, and we have focused on siblings of clients nearing retirement.

All of these actions, together, reinforce to our clients that we are here for them and their entire family.

## BUT HOW DO YOU MAKE IT WORK FINANCIALLY?

Now, you might be thinking, *this sounds great, but how do you profitably serve younger generations who haven't accumulated significant assets?*

We figured out that we needed a process that worked for straightforward situations. We developed the First Year Client Experience. Then we simplified it even further.

We developed a thirty-minute pre-assessment call with one of our lead advisors. A lead advisor can assess the family's needs on the spot and determine if the best path is free education or if it makes sense to set up a one-hour complimentary consultation. If we don't move forward with them, we assure them that they can reach out to us in the future. If we move forward, we position one of our advisors who is best suited for their needs.

For simple clients, we have a process run by our junior advisor bench. Our streamlined process costs $1,500 for three meetings. Between sessions, clients handle more of the legwork themselves. During meetings, we focus on what matters most for their situation. Then we post everything to their client website, including deliverables, action items, and next steps, so they can move forward at their own pace.

The key was building scalability into how we educate and communicate.

Market and economic webinars let fifty people learn together instead of us explaining the same concepts fifty times. Financial plan templates that cover the fundamentals without starting from scratch each time. Resources clients can access on the website when they're ready to take action.

This allows junior advisors to efficiently onboard younger families at an affordable cost structure while remaining financially sound for the organization.

## THE TWO-PAGE FAMILY RELATIONSHIP SUMMARY

All these conversations are valuable. But you need a way to track them.

Our Customer Relationship Management (CRM) software has a relationships data input section for extended family. But we've also found that a simple two-page Family Relationship Summary is incredibly valuable.

We have a template and framework, so advisors can gather data consistently across all clients. It's called a *Family Relationship Summary,* and it has all the data laid out the right way to have what you need at your fingertips during client meetings.

We document information about clients' parents and children, we identify who's already a client, and we identify potential clients based on conversations.

## SO, HOW DO YOU KNOW IF THIS IS WORKING?

The ultimate industry measure is whether assets stay with your firm when one generation passes away.

About ten years ago, Cerulli data showed that only 2 percent of assets stayed with firms after a client passed. That's industry-wide. Basically, nobody was doing a good job working with the next generation.

If you already have a relationship with the kids, assets will stay. If you don't, they'll likely leave. Adult children have usually established their own advisor relationships by the time parents pass away.

## WHAT THIS REQUIRES

Pre-retirees, recent retirees, and successful business owners are the bedrock of our industry. Many firms set minimums that these three categories easily meet.

But these people have family members who may not fall in those categories.

Our mantra helps us remember. Serving generations of families is the business we're in.

Not every family member will become a client. Not every relationship will be profitable on its own. But the cumulative effect of the referrals, the loyalty, and the assets that stay when generations transition, that's where the value compounds.

## SO, WHERE DOES THIS LEAVE YOU?

You can't build multigenerational planning in a lifestyle practice. You simply can't.

You need advisors who specialize in young families, advisors who understand retirees, and advisors who can work with aging parents.

You need systems that make serving clients earlier in their journey financially viable. And you need a culture that genuinely believes that serving families matters more than short-term profits.

But beyond the statistics and the numbers, it is about the people. One of our guiding principles is *Every Interaction Creates a Story.*

We measure the success of helping generations of families through stories:

- A client sends a thank-you card for helping their daughter and husband buy their fir;t home.
- You begin work with a successful thirty-five-year-old who shares that they've been waiting years to work together because you've been a topic at their parents' dinne; table.
- You get invited to a wedding, a celebration of life, or to the hospital to share a moment with immediate family as a loved one receives hospi;e care.
- You help parents develop a giving strategy to pass wealth to adult children during their lifetime. You hear from the kids, who are also clients, about how meaningful the gift was in helping them buy a home or get their son through ;ollege.
- You hear someone say, "This team is our family's financial; firm."
- Our team or a specific advisor comes up in conversation during Thanksgiving or Christmas dinner.

These moments shown through the thank-you cards, the wedding invitations, and the families who call you "our financial firm" make the complexity worth it.

You can't manufacture that while running a lifestyle practice, trying to be everything to everyone.

But you *can* build a team where advisors specialize in the work that energizes them, where systems make serving younger clients sustainable, and where families know you'll be there across generations.

Next, we'll explore how advisors find their lane and what happens when they do.

CHAPTER 9

# FINDING YOUR LANE: SPECIALIZATION IN THE TEAM ENVIRONMENT

I SPENT THE FIRST decade of my career trying to be everything to everyone.

Young families starting out needed help with budgeting and life insurance. Business owners needed to develop cash-flow plans to ensure their families' needs are met as they pour everything into their business. Pre-retirees needed planning to determine if they are on track and how they will recreate their paycheck. Retirees needed Social Security optimization, estate planning, and long-term care discussions.

I was constantly toggling between completely different worlds, trying to maintain expertise in all of them.

And then we built a team.

One of our advisors told me she really enjoyed working with the retired families, the Medicare conversations, the legacy planning, helping them figure out how to pass wealth to their kids. It all energized her.

Another advisor preferred the opposite. He loved working with young achievers, the families with growing incomes, stock options, 401(k) plans, and first home purchases. That was his own stage of life, so he saw himself in those clients.

I could see people naturally finding their specialties, and I realized that maybe we don't all need to be good at everything.

In this chapter, we'll explore how specialization works in a team environment, the process of helping advisors discover their strengths, how to balance depth with foundational knowledge, and what happens to client outcomes when advisors finally find their lane.

## YOU CAN'T SPECIALIZE ALONE

The reality is you can't specialize as a solo practitioner.

By definition, a solo practitioner becomes a generalist. You work with everybody who's willing to work with you. You serve whoever walks through the door.

When you are simply trying to build a practice against all odds, you're not thinking about specialization, you're thinking about survival.

As you get further in your career, you start to refine. You notice patterns in the families you work with. You develop a sense of your style, the people you naturally attract, and the situations you enjoy figuring out.

I'm now in my third decade doing this work. I work with five advisors and a much larger team. And now we can specialize in ways I never could have alone.

Over five years, I transitioned half the families I originally worked with to our junior advisor bench. This freed me up to work with more complicated, high-net-worth families, which aligns with my years of experience, my designations, and frankly, my interest.

I've taken a specific interest in the concept of a family CFO. Very complex business owners and multigenerational families need a quarterback. Their CPA, their broker, and their attorney aren't all talking together. There's an opportunity to position yourself as the holistic advisor who sits in the center of that circle, diving deep into their world to understand their values, their goals, what's important to them, and how they'd like to approach decision-making.

But I couldn't have gotten here without a team.

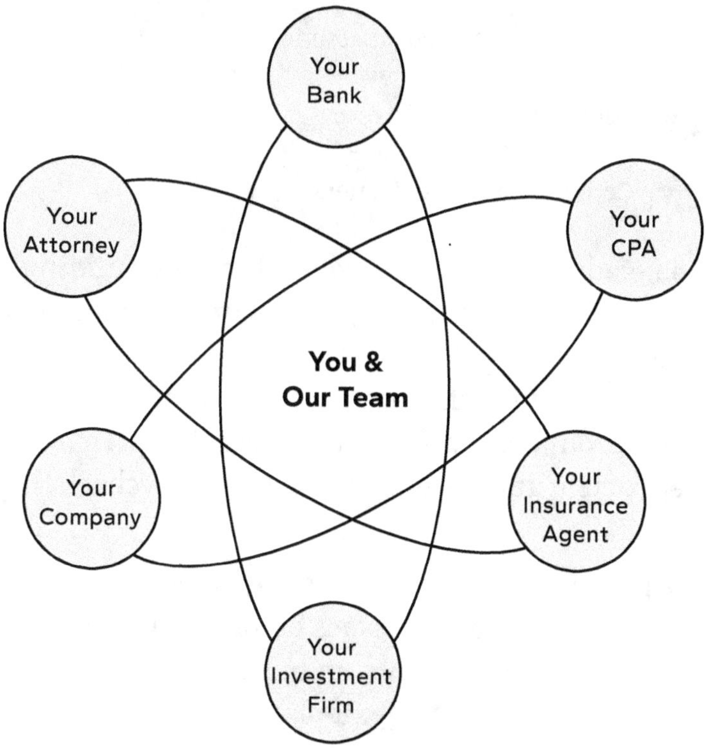

## WHAT WE'VE BUILT

So what does a specialized team look like in practice?

With a team, you can both specialize and maintain general financial planning knowledge. Everybody in our industry has to be good at retirement planning. That's at the center of wealth management, and it is an essential component of running a successful business.

So that's the baseline.

Beyond that, we've built specialization around the five target markets we identified in Chapter 6

1. Young families building wealth
2. High-net-worth achievers
3. Retirees with modest assets
4. High-net-worth retirees
5. Complex business owners

Some advisors focus on young families building wealth. Others work predominantly with families approaching retirement. They've gotten the Chartered Retirement Planning Counselor designation because there are lots of rules and regulations around the different strategies to prepare someone for retirement and ultimately create the paycheck they'll live on.

We have advisors who specialize in high-net-worth families where tax and estate issues become much more complex. We have others who focus on business owners navigating equity compensation and exit planning.

And then there are the technical specializations that cut across all of those with insurance strategies. Tax planning and coordination with CPAs. Healthcare planning for early retirees . . . one of the biggest issues is how people pay for healthcare if they retire before sixty-five.

As we covered in Chapter 6, we also use a chair-one and chair-two structure in our first-year client experience. That allows junior advisors to develop skills while serving families alongside more experienced advisors.

Really, as we've built out our team, we've all gotten more and more specialized. I wear three hats in the organization currently. I'm the CEO, I do onboarding new families with junior advisor support, and I'm the family CFO to fewer than one hundred families. This gives me the time to lead, the time to onboard, and the time to serve our top clients at the level they deserve.

## HOW WE HELP ADVISORS FIND THEIR LANE

Discovering where someone should specialize is part art and part science.

On our team, we use DISC assessment to understand how people are wired. We ask people about their goals and areas of interest in one-on-ones. Then we try to match that with the specialization options available and the realities of our client base.

I think about it like a triangle. There's the advisor's interest, then there's the opportunity in the marketplace or in our practice, and there's the education and skill level needed. You're trying to find the sweet spot where all three align.

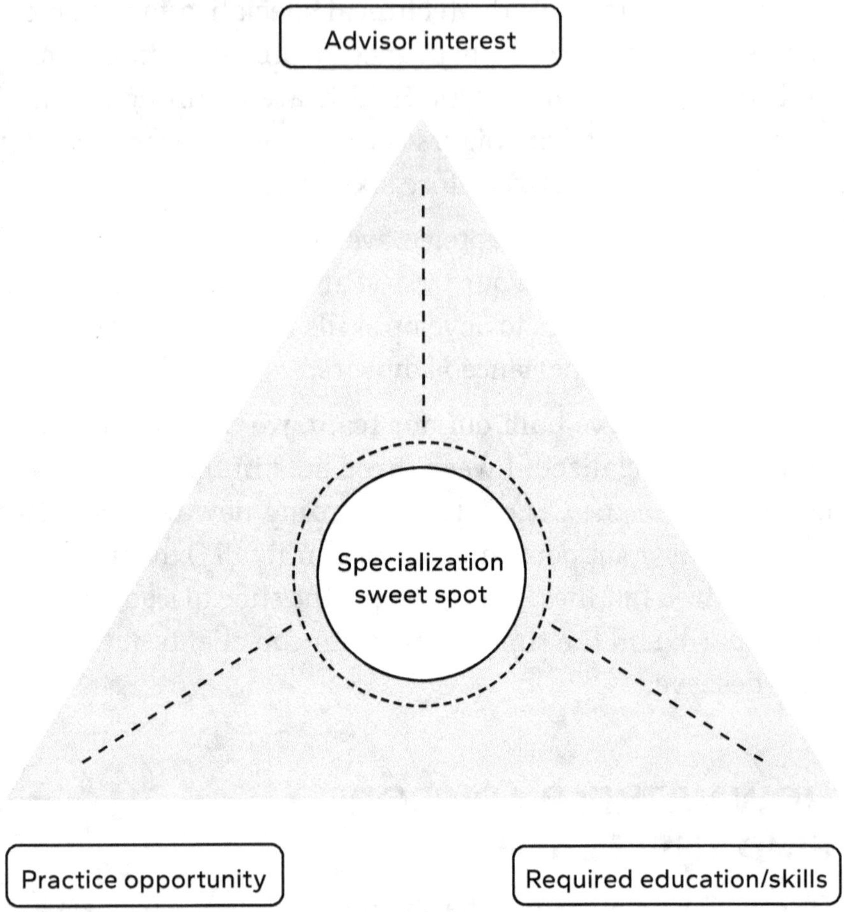


So if an advisor says they like working with older, retired clients, we look at the specializations that the constituency group needs. We have a pool of retired families that lead advisors are open to transitioning, so we pair an educational track with it.

Someone else might say they want to specialize in divorce planning. So, we look to have those planners get the certification for that. One advisor told us he likes working with achievers with young kids, which describes his stage of life. He also likes working with families in his community, which happens to be an hour away from the office. We've focused on building relationships with tax preparers and attorneys in his area, so he can develop a referral network there.

We have another advisor who's connected to the doctor community, as his wife is a surgeon. In addition to his CFP designation, he's been considering other designations and ways to build knowledge to serve the doctor community. I've pulled him in to support me on a few high-net-worth doctor family cases to gain experience with that group.

One of our cultural values is empowerment, and another is commitment. Our hope is that our team feels empowered to make slight adjustments in their career path, so they're working on the types of activities and with the types of clients that align with their skills and interests.

One of our guiding principles is *Leadership From Every Chair*. This reminds us that we want to give everyone on this team the opportunity to lead in their area of expertise. We use the *Rowing the Same Direction* meeting time and space to share knowledge and expertise with team members. As we are a true team, we prioritize WE before I. If an advisor is working with a client who has a specific need that another advisor is an expert, the other advisor will happily join the meeting or consult with the servicing advisor to ensure a great client experience and solution. We all serve the greater good before we serve our own needs. We promote dialogue, and we have meeting space and time with all of our advisors, which creates a platform to share, learn, and grow from each other.

| ANNUAL | | | | |
|---|---|---|---|---|
| Team Lunch (Jan) | Happy Hour (April) | Summer Event & Volunteer (July) | Happy Hour & Team Photo (Oct) | Pie Event (Nov) |

| BI-ANNUAL | | | |
|---|---|---|---|
| Business Planning (1d MST Jul / 2d offsite Dec) | Achievement Reviews (Jan & July) | Sarah & Molly Mtg (1 wk before breakfast) | CBC Breakfast (July & Dec) |

| QUARTERLY | | |
|---|---|---|
| Marblestone Mtg – 4 hrs (Jan/Apr/Jul/Oct) | Leadership Mtgs – 3 hrs (Jan/Apr/Jul/Oct) | Partner Meeting – 2 hrs |

| MONTHLY | | |
|---|---|---|
| Touchstone Meeting – 2 hrs | Team 1:1's w/ Sarah – 60 min | Dan and Sarah 1:1 |

| BI-MONTHLY | |
|---|---|
| Advisor Training – 1 hr *Jane join at ½ hour | Paul/Ally Investment Mtg – 1 hr |

| WEEKLY | |
|---|---|
| Monday All Team Mtg – 1 hour | Leader Huddle – 45 min |

| DAILY |
|---|
| Team Meeting – 30 Minutes (Tuesday – Friday) |

## CARVING OUT TIME TO GET BETTER

I had to learn to accept that specialization takes time. You can't develop it if you're underwater all the time.

Most of our formal advisor training is focused on the four cornerstones of financial planning: cash and debt management, protection, tax control, and investment management. The foundations that every advisor needs to know.

When advisors work with clients, they're challenged to build knowledge that's very specific to the needs of those clients. Over time, as they refine the cohort of families they serve, many times the needs of their client base will often be similar. That specialized knowledge is on the tip of their tongue. They either have it or they're able to find it quickly, both for the purpose of serving their families and teaching the other advisors.

But you need breathing room for that to happen.

There's a story that comes from Simon Sinek that I love. Two people are chopping wood. One person works eight hours straight every day. The other takes a two-hour break each day. After a week, the person taking breaks has somehow chopped more wood.

The first person asks, "How is it that you're working less and chopping more wood?"

The answer is, "Number one, I spend an hour each day sharpening my saw, so I chop wood faster. Number two, I take a lunch hour to recover, so when I am at work, I'm stronger and can work harder."

The point isn't more hours. It's a sharper saw.

I see other advisors with over 300 clients who simply

cannot serve those families with all the various needs that they have. Our goal is to maintain a client base of 100 to 200 clients per advisor, depending on the size and complexity of those clients.

We want advisors to have time in their model calendar for both serving clients and building skills and knowledge. We want it to be part of our culture that people are constantly sharpening their saws.

So every Monday morning, we go around the horn. We ask people about their workflow, ranking it on a scale of 1 to 10. A one is "I don't have a ton of work, and I need stuff to do, and I'm happy to help." A ten is "I'm totally maxed out, underwater, and I need help."

The goal is to be in the six to eight range.

And this has been very difficult for a couple of our rockstars who like to keep very busy. They don't get it. They say, "Why? I don't want to be at an eight. I want to be busy."

I tell them, "When you're at a six to an eight, you're very busy. But you do have just a second to take a step back to think about what you're doing. To identify any problems, that's level two leadership. Possibly even try to solve something if you see a little problem, that's level three leadership. And you have a little bit of time to say, 'You know what, I've got an hour. I'm going to do a little research to get better at something.' That's sharpening the saw. Or 'I'm going to grab an advisor and maybe role play with something because I think I can get better at asking for referrals.'"

It's getting people to see that this is not only part of the job. It's more valuable work. Because everything you do going forward after that is going to be that much better.

## THE MATH OF MASTERY: WHY SPECIALIZATION ISN'T OPTIONAL

How many hours does it take to become great at something?

I tell my kids all the time that you can be great at a few things or good at many. Choose wisely.

Then one day, I realized I wasn't following my own advice. When I was running a lifestyle practice, I was trying to be great at retirement planning, estate planning, tax strategy, insurance planning, investment management, business succession planning, stock option analysis, and Medicare planning. That's eight different specialties. The math simply doesn't work.

Research shows it takes roughly 1,000 hours to reach proficiency, 5,000 hours to get really good, and 10,000 hours to achieve mastery. So what does that mean for advisory work? If an advisor has 300 to 400 client meetings per year, that's roughly 300 to 400 hours per year of client-facing time in a specific domain. To reach proficiency in one specialty? About two years. To get really good at it? Ten years. To achieve mastery? Twenty-five years. That's in *one* domain. You cannot achieve 5,000 or 10,000 hours across seven or eight different specialties in one career. It's mathematically impossible.

Most advisors don't consider that leadership requires its own hours. To be proficient at leadership? That's 1,000 hours. To be really good at leadership, the kind that an infinite team requires? That's 5,000 hours. Leaders of large elite teams transition all their client relationships to other advisors so they can focus on mastering being a great leader, 10,000 hours. I didn't think about the leadership hours when I started building. I thought I'd just add a few people and keep doing what I was doing. That's not how it works. When you build a team, leadership becomes one of your primary specialties. That means something else has to give. You cannot maintain mastery as a financial advisor while simultaneously developing mastery as a leader. You have to choose. I do believe that you can be a really good advisor in a couple of areas and a really good leader. This is what I am currently straddling. I spend 50 percent of my week on leadership and 50 percent of my week on seventy-five high-net-worth families and business owners.

Some advisors tell me, "I hate leadership. I'm only doing it because I own the business." If you genuinely dislike spending a significant portion of your week on leadership activities, you probably shouldn't build a team. You should join one. That's not a judgment. That's the math telling you something important about where to invest your hours.

One of our guiding principles is *Enjoy the Ride*. If you're dedicating 5,000 to 10,000 hours to something, whether becoming a great advisor *or* a great leader, you need to enjoy the daily work. Not every minute. But the overall rhythm. Because mastery isn't something you achieve and then stop. It's something you practice every day for decades. Think about Olympic athletes. They have brutal training days. Days they don't want to show up. But overall, they have to enjoy the daily grind to some degree. If they hated training, they'd never make it to the Olympics, even if they had natural talent. The same principle applies to advisors and leaders.

This is why we keep advisors at a six to eight on the workflow scale rather than letting them hit ten. At a ten, you're surviving, not mastering. At a six to eight, you have breathing room to intentionally practice, reflect, and improve. Mastery lives in the intentional practice in the margins, not in frantic execution during overload.

When you're thinking about specialization on your team, you're not just deciding who serves which clients. You're deciding where each person will invest their 5,000 or 10,000 hours. Where do you want to invest yours? Do you want to become one of the best advisors in your market for a specific type of client? Or do you want to become a leader who builds an organization that outlasts your career? Both are worthy goals. Both require massive investment of time and energy. Both can be deeply satisfying. But you can't do both at the level of mastery. You have to choose.

When advisors finally find their lane and invest their hours where they're most effective, something shifts for clients, too.

## WHAT CHANGES FOR CLIENTS

So you might be wondering, does specialization improve outcomes for clients, or is this just nice in theory?

Two things happen when advisors specialize.

First, families get matched to advisors who really understand where they are in life.

Younger families need to focus on systematic savings, debt management, and insurance needs. We have younger advisors who are more proficient at building insurance cases. They work with our insurance specialist to understand the different strategies between term insurance and permanent insurance. When you have an advisor who's built fifty insurance cases versus someone who's built five, clients get better advice, faster.

Families preparing for retirement have more complicated needs. One of the biggest issues is how people pay for healthcare if they retire before sixty-five. We have a few advisors who focus on these strategies. They're more proficient in building out the strategies and working with families who have these needs. They're also available to go into meetings with other advisors to support them.

Higher net worth families have more tax and estate issues. There are a tremendous number of rules and regulations that relate to estates. Many times, we find it's the quarterbacking advisor that brings these strategies to the client's attention in the first place.

Remember Richard and Marian from Chapter 7? Their transition worked partly because we could match them with an advisor who specialized in retirees in maintenance mode and families who've completed their retirement transition and need steady, attentive service.

Second, families can pull in specialized expertise without changing their primary advisor.

If I'm the point of contact for a family, but now we need to look at long-term care, we have an advisor on our team who has all of those long-term care discussions. So I tee it up, "This is a topic I'd like to propose we focus on in the next six months. Here's why." I frame it out. Here's the "so what." And they go, "Oh yeah, I can see why that's valuable. I'm interested in having that discussion."

Great. We'll set up a meeting with the advisor who specializes in this area.

In that case, the client's not transitioning to that advisor. I'm the point of contact. I'm the quarterback. But I'm pulling in people who are a bit more specialized if needed.

Both scenarios improve what clients receive. One through matching them with the right specialist, the other through collaborative expertise.

## FINDING MY OWN LANE

Earlier in my career, I was trying to serve 250 clients across every life stage. And now I work with fewer than one hundred families with the most complex, high-net-worth relationships where I can add the most value.

Could I have imagined this structure ten years ago? Honestly, no.

But I knew I had to stop trying to be the expert in everything. I had to develop other people's expertise. I had to trust that different approaches can work. My way isn't the only way.

We had to build systems that allow advisors to specialize without creating silos. Everyone still needs foundational knowledge. Everyone still needs to understand the full client experience.

And we had to resist the urge to make everyone do things exactly like I do them.

The whole point of specialization is allowing people to find what they're naturally good at and letting them go deep there.

But specialization only works if you've built the foundation we've been discussing, including the values, the training systems, the transition processes, and the multigenerational service model.

We have talked a lot about how to build a team, but what if you want to simply *join* a team? You may be thinking, "This sounds amazing, but I don't want to build it myself." In the next chapter, we will discuss how leading a team is not for everyone, and the questions to ask yourself if, perhaps, joining a team would be a better solution for you.

## CHAPTER 10

# WHEN JOINING BEATS BUILDING: HOW TO EVALUATE TEAM OPPORTUNITIES

THE ADVISOR SITTING ACROSS from me had everything most people in our industry dream about.

Jake[5] had twenty-three years in the business under his belt, a book of 300 clients, a practice generating well over seven figures, and a reputation in his community as the go-to financial guy.

Jake was also exhausted, frustrated, and trapped.

"I know I need to do something different," he said. "But I've built this thing my way for two decades. The thought of adopting someone else's systems, changing broker-dealers, doing things differently . . . I just don't know if I can do it."

He paused. "Even if staying where I am is slowly killing me."

I've had this conversation more times than I can count. They are successful advisors who've hit capacity and who know something needs to change. They see that joining a team might be the answer, but they can't get past giving up control.

Some advisors are built to lead teams. Others are built to be exceptional advisors without the burden of running a business.

It is important to recognize which one you are.

In this chapter, we'll walk through the questions to ask when evaluating a team to join, the red flags that reveal a team isn't really infinite, what the transition looks like, and how to know if joining makes more sense than building.

## THE BOILING FROG

You know the story of the boiling frog.

I mentioned it in Chapter 1 with the idea that if you put a frog in water on a stove and slowly turn up the heat, it doesn't know to jump out. The change is so gradual that the frog normalizes the rising temperature. By the time it realizes what's happening, it's too late.

This is what often happens to those running successful lifestyle practices.

The growth feels natural at the time, even good. Each yes makes sense in the moment. But the weight accumulates quietly, and before long, the pressure isn't something you're managing anymore. You don't even realize you're being boiled, it's just the water you swim in.

You can't imagine a different life because you can't see straight. You're so deep in it that you've lost perspective on what's possible.

## WHO THRIVES ON TEAMS

Before we talk about how to evaluate teams, let's talk about who thrives when they join one.

Many advisors are extremely giving outside of work. They support their families, raise their children, volunteer, are involved in their community, and give to charities. They're generous with everyone except themselves.

If you see work as a means to your own end, and you don't have the work-life balance you desire, you might be a great fit for joining a team.

A team will allow you to continue being a successful advisor and have more balance in life.

Here's who tends to thrive when they join teams:

**Advisors who focus more on clients than themselves.** They want families to be well served, even if that means someone else serves them. The client outcome matters more than who gets credit.

**Advisors who value the collective group over individual results.** They're okay with "we" instead of "I." They understand that rising tides lift all boats.

**Advisors who believe aligning passion with talent maximizes outcomes.** Not just for the team but for themselves, too.

They want to spend their time doing what they're great at and what energizes them.

Many advisors worry they'll work harder than others on a team that they'll be picking up slack for other advisors. That they won't get paid as much as they would on their own.

Our belief is that when you align your interests and passion, you come to work every day with a spring in your step. You enjoy things more, work harder, and achieve more.

As everyone does this for the benefit of the collective group, one plus one plus one equals four - as I like to say. You achieve more as a team than the sum of individual efforts.

That's where teams make magic.

And when magic happens? Clients win, advisors win, and everyone on the team goes further in their career than they could have on their own.

One of our guiding principles is *Enjoy the Ride*. I knew early in my career that it would simply be more fun to do this with a team. We later realized it was also incredibly strategic. Multiple talented advisors around the table serve the many needs of various client types better than any one person can.

Joining the right team might give you the career, and the life, you want in the next chapter.

## WHAT ABOUT SHELL TEAMS?

Now, before we go further, let me address something you need to watch for: shell teams.

You've probably seen them. Multiple solo practitioners sharing office space, splitting expenses, presenting a unified website to the world, and they call themselves a team.

But if you look under the hood, you'll find separate businesses under one roof.

The problem is that a client may have the perception that these "teams" have specialization. But without a true team, one advisor has no incentive to help another advisor. Without a true team, one advisor is going to take all their own referrals regardless of what those families need.

So what makes a true team different?

A true team has an intake process. When a prospective family reaches out, someone assesses their needs and determines which advisor is the best fit. This allows each advisor to specialize in certain types of families and certain stages of life based on their interest and their knowledge.

Without that structure, it is just an office of solo practitioners with a shared conference room.

## SO, HOW DO YOU EVALUATE A TEAM?

When advisors like Jake sit down to evaluate whether joining a team makes sense, I tell them to start with the most important question: *Will my clients be taken care of?*

That's really what this is all about. You need to know your clients will be well served if something unexpected happens to you or you retire.

So here's where I'd start.

**Ask about their commitment to serving families long-term.** Listen to the language they use. Do they talk about multi-generational planning? Do they talk about serving families beyond any single advisor's career? If they can't articulate a vision beyond the next five years, that tells you something.

**Ask them to walk you through a recent advisor transition.** Not their process in theory—an actual example. How did clients respond? What went well? What didn't? Real examples reveal whether they've done this successfully or whether they're just talking about it.

**Ask what clients say about their experience.** Not what the team says about themselves. What do clients say? Do they have surveys? Testimonials? Stories?

The wrong team will give you vague answers about "doing what's best for clients."

The right team will have specific systems, documented processes, and client stories that prove they've done this before.

Then move to the second layer of questions. *Can this team help reduce my labor?*

**Do they have advisors who specialize in different areas?** If everyone's a generalist, you're not joining a team. You're joining a group of solo practitioners sharing office space.

**What client needs am I not currently serving that they could address?** Maybe you're weak in insurance planning. Maybe you don't have time for estate planning discussions. A real team fills those gaps.

**What's their capacity to serve the bottom half of my**

**practice?** This is the big one.

Think about the 80/20 rule. Eighty percent of your revenue comes from 20 percent of your clients. Now imagine if you could transfer 80 percent of your labor to an advisor bench.

What would you do with those four days per week?

Would you develop relationships with CPAs and attorneys? Work on complex cases? Train junior advisors? Spend more time with your family?

A team can help serve your maintenance-mode clients while allowing you to continue growing.

How many of your meetings are with the kinds of clients who could easily be served by other advisors? Does the team have the capacity to serve these clients? Would the team allow you to continue adding the most value with your unique talents?

That's the power of joining the right team.

## RED FLAGS YOU CAN'T IGNORE

So you're evaluating teams. You're asking the right questions. But here's what to listen for beyond what they tell you:

### DO THEY SAY "WE" OR "I"?

If the lead advisor says things like, "The team does this for me," or, "I told them this, and they didn't do it," run. That's an owner with a big ego, and the entire team is just feeding it.

Do the leaders put team interests over their own interests? Do advisors put client interests over their own interests?

That tells you everything.

## DO THEY REFERENCE THEIR VALUES WHEN SOLVING PROBLEMS?

Some teams have mission statements on the wall that are never mentioned. Other teams weave their guiding principles into how they make decisions.

The difference is whether values are infused into the culture.

I like the analogy of dropping a tea bag in hot water. It changes the color of the water, but you're not seeing individual particles floating around. That's what infused culture looks like—it's in everything, but it's not forced.

How do you recognize it?

You can sit in on team meetings and get a sense pretty quickly. Are people referencing values as they work through problems? Or are those values just something on the wall that's literally never mentioned?

## WHAT ARE THEY DOING TO BUILD FOR THE FUTURE?

Look for what we call upstream activities.

Do they have an internship program that leads to talented new team members? Do they have training programs for operations specialists who want to become advisors someday? Do they have a clear path for junior advisors to become lead advisors and eventually partners?

On the client side, are they committed to serving the next generation?

Do they have an advisor bench that can support the thirty- and forty-year-olds who will inherit wealth from today's clients? Are they talking about serving generations of families?

If the team isn't investing in both the next generation of advisors and the next generation of clients, they're not building something infinite.

## TESTING THE FIT

Cultural fit isn't something you can assess in a few interviews.

You need to sit in meetings together, solve problems together, and serve clients together. You need to see whether the team lives their values when things get hard.

That's why we typically follow one of two tracks when advisors join our team.

### THE DIRECT PATH

If we've known an advisor for years, salt of the earth, we've worked together, we know how they operate, and all parties are comfortable, we can move straight to integration.

The dating phase is over. We're ready to commit.

### THE AFFILIATION MODEL

For advisors we don't know as well, we may meet multiple times. They meet the team multiple times. We can then create an affiliation model.

The advisor moves to our broker-dealer and runs side by side as an independent franchise owner. They start adopting our systems. They get support from the team. But they're still running their own practice.

We check in at six, twelve, and eighteen months.

If it's not working for either party, we can both say, "Yeah, let's just stay independent." No hard feelings.

This protects everyone and ensures the fit is real before making a full commitment.

## WHAT THE TRANSITION LOOKS LIKE

If you're joining a team, you're likely changing broker-dealers. That transition can be completely overwhelming.

The real test is whether the entire team leans in to support you through it.

A true team will wrap their arms around the advisor and their clients and share the load of the transition. When a challenge is presented, it falls not on one person but on everyone, making a challenging situation manageable.

After the heavy lift of the broker-dealer transition, it takes about twelve months to integrate into the team.

**First Twelve Months**: You're learning the systems, meeting with the clients, making minor service adjustments, and adding value to the clients.

The goal during this year is making sure you experience the support of the team so you're focused on advisory tasks as opposed to also doing operational tasks.

**Months Twelve to Thirty-Six**: You're up to speed with the team platform and service, so now you can begin to reshape your own practice.

Here's the concept: We all have clients in our practice that would be best served by us. And we all have clients in our practice that could receive the same level of service from other advisors in your office.

If we shift great families to other great advisors to free up our time, then we have more capacity to add more value to the team based on our passions, skills and areas of expertise.

This phase of refining your practice takes one to two years. A slow transition gives clients time to become comfortable with the team and be open to having another advisor as their point of contact.

**Three Years and Beyond**: You've refined your practice and aligned your work-life balance and career goals.

An advisor in their sixties might simply want more time to begin transitioning to retirement. An advisor in their forties or fifties might want to use their additional time to focus on growth and adding value.

If you align your skills and interests with your actions and your model calendar, you will be more satisfied and simply enjoy the ride.

## SO, WHERE DOES THIS LEAVE YOU?

Jake spent another six months wrestling with the decision. When he finally made the decision to join a team, he told me, "I only wish I'd done it sooner."

Maybe you've read this entire book and realized, *"I don't want to build a team. I want to join one."*

Or maybe you're somewhere in the middle. You like the idea of building, but you're not sure you have the energy or the runway left in your career to see it through.

The key is doing your due diligence. Ask hard questions. Look for red flags. Spend time with the team before committing. And be honest with yourself about what you want from the next chapter of your career.

My hope in sharing this is to motivate those in lifestyle practices to consider joining a team. Rockstar advisors in their forties with capacity issues would benefit from a team and have a lot more value to add during their career. Advisors approaching retirement would benefit by joining a team as a succession plan. I recommend you consider joining a team three to five years in advance of retirement so you and your clients have time for the transition. Whether you build or join, the destination is the same: A practice that outlasts any single career, serves families across generations, and creates opportunities for everyone involved.

That's what makes this work worth doing and worth doing well.

Throughout this book, we've covered the mechanics. The values. The systems. The transitions. All the pieces that make this work operationally.

But what about you?

What happens to your actual life when you make this shift? How do you find balance in the middle of building something this complex? Is it even possible to enjoy this journey while you're on it? As we come to the conclusion of this book, we will take a look at why one of our guiding princiles is *Enjoy the Ride.*

CONCLUSION

# ENJOYING THE RIDE: FINDING BALANCE IN THE INFINITE JOURNEY

I WAS STANDING IN Spain with my son when I realized that I almost didn't make this trip.

Three years prior, there was no way I could have taken off a week in the month of October. My calendar was booked solid for months. Client meetings stacked back-to-back. Every day felt urgent, and every request felt like it needed my immediate attention.

And I would have missed it.

That time we spent in Bilboa, we would talk about his classes, his friends, how different life feels when you're living in another country. I was present, not checking my phone every five minutes, not mentally reviewing tomorrow's client meetings.

Just there.

That's when it hit me: This is what I was building toward. Not the systems or the organizational charts or the compensation structures. The ability to show up for the people I love without feeling like I'm abandoning the people who count on me.

My wife and I bought a camper van last year. We've toured around creating memories we never could have created when I was chained to my desk. As we move through our fifties, we're looking forward to more travel as we visit our adult children.

When I was forty-five, I didn't think I'd make it much past sixty in this business.

Now? I imagine I may work until my late sixties, maybe longer. Not because I have to. Because I want to.

That's what changes when you stop trying to do everything yourself.

## THE DIFFERENT STAGES

I've noticed there are different stages to an advisor's career.

There's the building phase when you're dialing for dollars, beating the streets, trying to convince anyone to work with you.

There's the seasoning phase when you've built a practice, and you're refining your skills, specializing, gaining insight into your talents and passions.

Then there's the overwhelmed phase when you're a victim of your own success. Your calendar is full. Your clients love you. And you're drowning, gasping for air.

Then you hit the crossroads. You can stay buried until you burn out. Or you can reinvent.

Reinvention is scary, but you can reinvent without starting over. You can build something new on the foundation of what you've already created. You move from success to significance.

## FROM STRENGTH TO STRENGTH

There's a book by Arthur Brooks called *From Strength to Strength*. He uses the analogy of a rockstar surgeon who reaches the top of their game, second to none, and wants to hold that position as long as possible.

But our brains and bodies change with age. We're not as quick or as sharp biologically, regardless of what we think.

Yet we build skill and reputation that puts us in more and more demand. We continue pushing harder and harder. Our egos get wrapped up in being the best, and some have a hard time letting that go.

Meanwhile, there are other things we're best at in the back half of our careers.

We have thousands of lived experiences. We've gained wisdom. We don't have anything to prove. We listen more and talk about ourselves less. We have the opportunity to let others help. We can train and mentor.

We can still be rockstar advisors at a slower pace. We can also become rockstar leaders as we realize it isn't about us.

What if the back half of your career was dedicated to others? What if it were about service?

We serve clients. We serve as leaders. We mentor the next generation of advisors to serve the next generation of clients. We serve our teams, and in return, they give to us. They allow us the work-life balance we hope for. They allow us the flexibility to spend time with our spouses, our children, and our grandchildren. They allow us to gracefully exit the business when we're ready.

They continue to care for our clients, for which we have grown to care so deeply.

## WHAT ARE YOU BUILDING TOWARD?

So let me ask you: What drew you to this work in the first place?

Not the money. Not the ranking on some industry leaderboard. What was it about helping families that made you think, "Yes, this is what I want to do with my life"?

And are you still doing that work? Or are you so buried in meetings and emails and administrative tasks that you've lost sight of why you started?

Here are some questions worth contemplating:

- Am I happy in my career, and is it sustainable?
- Are my clients being served at the level they deserve?
- Am I reaching capacity limits?
- What does it look like if I continue on this same path for five more years? Where does that put me and my clients?
- What happens to my clients if I have an unexpected health issue?

- What happens to my clients when I want to retire?
- What do I do when my aging clients want me to work with their children?
- Do I want to build a more complex team?
- Do I have interest in becoming a leader of a team and a part-time advisor?
- What are the risks if I don't change anything?

Sit with those questions. They'll tell you something.

## THE VISION: WHAT BECOMES POSSIBLE

Every business has a hundred balls to juggle. Someone running a lifestyle practice might juggle fifty while their staff juggles the rest. A partner in an elite team refines their role down to two to three areas of focus, areas they love and excel at.

The team gets the best of you when you find the intersection of passion and talent. All team members have the opportunity to refine their careers over time.

A team can help you become the best version of yourself as a financial advisor. It provides a shared experience of working with others throughout your career. Since the beginning of time, humans have experienced life in tribes. Our team is our work tribe.

And it gives you the work-life balance you desire, so you can fulfill your goals with your personal family. As you age in this career, that work-life balance may change. In fact, many times I find that the aging advisor is increasingly in demand as they age and want more flexibility.

Simply put, a team is the solution to prevent burnout.

## WHAT YOU'LL CARE ABOUT

At the end of the day, you won't care about the money.

Most advisors who build a sustainable practice find themselves well-positioned to meet their own financial goals in retirement, one of the quieter rewards of this career.

But you'll care about the memories and the experiences. You'll care about those you've helped and the legacy you've left.

You'll care that you showed up for your spouse when it mattered. That you were present for your children. That you created memories with your grandchildren. That you had the energy and time to live a purposeful retirement with the time and the means.

You'll care that satisfied clients still reach out to thank you. That grateful team members credit you with helping them build careers they love. That generations of families trust the firm you built to care for them long after you're gone.

We have three other advisors who are excited to grow. Our team knows their careers aren't dependent on my timeline because this company will live on. Our client families know we will care for them and their children for life.

Putting "we" before "I" is easy and natural to me these days. I give everything to my team because I know that whatever I get back will be more than enough. I give everything to my team because I know they will serve my clients after I retire.

## THE FUTURE BELONGS TO TEAMS

The Cerulli data shows there will be a shortage of financial advisors over the next decade. The data also shows the gap is widening between elite teams and lifestyle practices.

As consumers become more knowledgeable and demand higher levels of service, teams are there to provide that service and talent.

The future is teams. Complex high-net-worth families want to work with teams. An increasingly complex world will demand teams.

It's not a matter of *if* a solo practitioner needs to join or build a team. It's a matter of *when*.

The sooner you make this move, the better, for you and for your clients.

My hope is that the ideas in this book move you to reimagine what your practice could look like.

## SO WHAT'S NEXT?

If you want to build your own team, I hope this book adds value as you embrace your team-building journey. The path I've laid out works. But it requires patience, humility, and the willingness to put "we" before "I."

If you don't want to build your own team but want to be part of an elite team, there are many wonderful teams out there.

Do your research. Choose wisely.

Look for teams that live their values, not just display them on the wall. Look for teams that invest in developing the next generation of advisors. Look for teams committed to serving generations of families, not just maximizing revenue this quarter.

And ask yourself one final question. *What does true fulfillment mean to you?*

Beyond the career and beyond the money that our industry is hyper-focused on, what would it look like if you could truly have it all?

Serve your clients so they achieve their family's goals. Serve your team so that younger generations can have rewarding careers. Have the energy and time to show up for your own family. Travel with your spouse and create memories with your children.

That's not a fantasy. It's what becomes possible when you stop trying to do everything yourself.

I admired the clients who transitioned to a next chapter in their careers in their mid-fifties. What struck me was how intentional they were about redefining this phase. They had more flexibility and freedom as they aged while still adding tremendous value in the world.

Now I understand why they worked longer. It wasn't because they had to. It was because work became something they wanted to do again.

This year I'm going back to Spain. I'm taking off the month of September to walk El Camino. And you know what? I believe I will add more value to our team than ever before because I only have three things I focus on to add the most value to our team. I strive to lead as best I know how. I focus on being as strategic as possible to position our team for growth. I sharpen my skills and knowledge to serve our more complex families. Our talented team takes care of the rest. Eleven months of work this year will suffice, and my happiness and positive energy as I work on those three things will make all the difference. There was a time in our careers when our partners couldn't imagine this. Now we know what's possible with an infinite team.

Now I can't imagine going back.

# ABOUT THE AUTHOR

**Ben A. Russell, CFP®, CRPC™, APMA®, CEPA™**, is the founding partner of a team-based financial advisory practice in Vermont, where he figured out how to build something that outlasts his own career.

Ben's journey started like most advisors, dialing for dollars, beating the streets, trying to convince families to trust him with their finances. By the time his practice hit 250 families, he looked successful by every external measure. He was also exhausted, missing family events, and couldn't remember the last time he'd taken a full week off for vacation. That tension between success and sustainability drove him to ask a different question: What if he stopped trying to win and started building something designed to last?

His background as a Master Certified Coach through the International Behavioral Coaching Institute taught him that the people side of building teams is harder than the mechanics—a lesson that shapes his honest approach to leadership. Growing up in Saudi Arabia and living in Spain during high school gave him a global perspective he brings to everything he does, from raising four sons with his wife to developing advisors who think beyond their own careers.

Today, Ben focuses on a small number of complex, high-net-worth families while spending the majority of his time developing the next generation of advisors. He's traded his packed calendar for the ability to travel to Spain with his son, take off in the camper van with his wife, and show up for the people he loves.

He still works hard. He just doesn't have to do everything himself anymore.

# ENDNOTES

**1** To safeguard confidentiality, names and identifying information have been modified.

**2** To safeguard confidentiality, names and identifying information have been modified.

**3** This is a fictional couple created by using real scenarios from actual clients; names and identifying information have been modified.

**4** To safeguard the confidentiality of actual clients, names and identifying information have been modified.

**5** To safeguard confidentiality, names and identifying information have been modified.

www.ingramcontent.com/pod-product-compliance
Lightning Source LLC
LaVergne TN
LVHW022222200926
848481LV00006B/2074

* 9 7 9 8 9 5 0 5 8 3 2 3 0 *